THOMAS CROMWELL

A HISTORICAL SOURCEBOOK

HERITAGE HUNTER

Preface, chronology, introductory passages, selection and design

© Heritage Hunter, 2020, all rights reserved.

http://www.heritagehunter.co.uk

ISBN 978-1-905315-72-7

No part of this book may be reproduced in any form or by any electronic or mechanical means, including information storage and retrieval systems, without written permission from the publisher, except for the use of brief quotations in a book review.

With thanks to Andrea Scarpetta for assistance with Latin translation.

In CROMWELL thou hast the Example of a new Man's fortune, made great by Arts of Court, and reach of a shrewd Wit, upon the advantages of a corrupt Prince, and Times; shewing, that nothing is certaine in newnesse, where the Creature's Fall may in some measure deliver the mortall Creator from the envie of his proper Acts, and Insolencies.

— MICHAEL DRAYTON

My prayer is that God give me no longer life than I shall be glad to use mine office in edification, and not in destruction.

— THOMAS CROMWELL, 1538

CONTENTS

PREFACE

Interest in Thomas Cromwell has never been greater than in the last decade, fuelled by Hilary Mantel's bestselling *Wolf Hall* and *Bring up the Bodies* (and now the final part, *The Mirror and the Light*), as well as well-regarded biographies. And in the last few decades, rather than simply seeing him as a Machiavellian villain, historians have come to adopt a more nuanced view of his contribution to 16th century politics.

At some point all of these writers will have needed to turn to the contemporary sources for Cromwell's life – and indeed will have found that they are not extensive, or at least many of them follow a path of Chinese whispers, one chronicler echoing another, from only a few years after Cromwell's death until well into the 17th century.

Hitherto those principal sources have not been gathered together – hence this volume, which encompasses the few direct discussions of Cromwell's biography during his lifetime, some writings of his own, and the initial chain of chroniclers who offered their own interpretations of his life and work. One of the most influential, for example, was Foxe's *Book of Martyrs* (see Chapter 20), but even this drew significantly upon Bandello's *Novelle* – with that ostensibly a form of fiction. And we must remember these works were produced in a time when precision of historical scholarship was rare or barely considered. But in all of these there are nuggets of truth – and inevitably they also reveal in interesting, varied ways how history and biography are always in the eye of the beholder.

The significant omission in this collection is the vast amount of Cromwell's correspondence, let alone letters about him (though particularly interesting samples of both, from friends and from foes, are nonetheless here), which survives in the *Letters and Papers of Henry VIII* (see Bibliography). There are countless letters which reveal tiny slivers of Cromwell's movements or doings, and which his biographers have combed through. The intention here, though, is to offer the longer passages about him, in order to give a broader flavour of the man.

Three appendices also consider the earliest 'fictional' treatments of his life (other than Bandello's in Chapter 17), one from someone who actually knew Cromwell, and the others from a couple of generations later. The success of Hilary Mantel's trilogy, and many other intermediate works which feature Cromwell in one way or another (from Shakespeare's *Henry VIII* onwards), show that he is destined to remain a character of great fascination.

Note on the text: The original texts here have come from a variety of sources, hence some have been transcribed into more modern English, and some are in the original 15th century style; in some cases minor editing has been done for clarity.

THOMAS CROMWELL: A BIOGRAPHICAL CHRONOLOGY

c.1485

Thomas Cromwell was born in Putney, Surrey, the son of Walter Cromwell (also, it seems, known as Walter Smyth) – a blacksmith, fuller and cloth merchant, as well as owner of both a hostelry and a brewery – and Katherine Maverell, who had Derbyshire connections. Katherine lived in Putney in the house of a local attorney, John Welbeck, at the time of her marriage to Walter Cromwell in 1474. Cromwell elder sister, Katherine, later married Morgan Williams, a Welsh lawyer; his younger sister, Elizabeth, married a farmer, William Wellyfed. Katherine and Morgan's son, Richard, was employed in his uncle's service and changed his name to Cromwell (and was the direct ancestor of Oliver Cromwell).

1500–1510

Cromwell travelled to Italy. By some accounts, he joined the French army as a mercenary and fought against the Italians in the Battle of Garigliano (28 December 1503) – although, as with many details of his early biography, this has been disputed, and records of Thomas and

Walter Smyth suggest he could not have travelled until 1504. While in Italy, Cromwell apparently entered service in the household of the Florentine banker Francesco Frescobaldi, who rescued him off the Florentine streets, where he was starving after leaving the French mercenaries, according to Bandello's account (see Chapter 17).

1512

A letter written to Cromwell many years later suggests he may have been trading at Middelburgh in the Netherlands, or at least working as a secretary to English merchants; Cardinal Pole (see Chapter 11) also indicates that Cromwell had been a clerk to a Venetian merchant in this decade. *The Complete Peerage* (1889 edition) also suggests that he was already established as a lawyer and cloth-dresser in London by 1513.

1514

Cromwell is recorded as staying at the English Hospital in Rome in June of this year. He may have worked for the then Archbishop of York, Christopher Bainbridge (succeeded by Thomas Wolsey), as a collector of revenues.

c.1515

Cromwell married Elizabeth Wyckes. She was the widow of Thomas Williams, a Yeoman of the Guard, and the daughter of a Putney shearman, Henry Wykes, who had served as a gentleman usher to Henry VII.

1516

From sometime around 1516 Cromwell became a member of the household of Cardinal Wolsey, who had been Archbishop of York since 1514 and Lord High Chancellor of England since 1515.

1517–18

In 1517, and again in 1518, Cromwell led an embassy to Rome to obtain from Pope Leo X a papal bull for the reinstatement of Indulgences for the town of Boston, Lincolnshire.

1519

By this time Cromwell was possibly a member of Wolsey's council.

1520

Cromwell was also now firmly established in London mercantile and legal circles, advising Wolsey and other members of the nobility on legal and financial matters. Cromwell's son Gregory was born around 1520.

1522

Although Cromwell's main work was as a solicitor, there is some suggestion that he might also have been working in the family business of cloth-dressing. Cromwell's daughter Anne may have been born in this year.

1523

Cromwell became a burgess in the House of Commons, under Wolsey's patronage, although his constituency is unknown. The Calendar of Henry VIII suggests he was then 'dwelling by Fenchurch in London'. His daughter Grace is believed to have been born in this year.

1524

At some point in 1524 Cromwell has moved home to Austin Friars (also known as Augustine Friars, in the City of London), 'against the gate of the Friars' (see Stow, Chapter 22), where he remained for a decade. In this year he was elected a member of Gray's Inn and was acting formally as Wolsey's solicitor. He was also appointed Commissioner for the Subsidy for London.

1525

On 4 January, Cromwell was appointed as Wolsey's agent to investigate the wealth of five small monasteries.

1525–30

The investigation of monasteries by Cromwell continued with 29 being dissolved to raise funds for Wolsey; these were used to found the King's School in Ipswich in 1528 and Cardinal College, Oxford in 1529 (later refounded twice, eventually becoming Christ Church College in 1546). In 1527 Cromwell and Wolsey sought evidence to support Henry VIII's desire for a divorce from Catherine of Aragon, encouraged by Henry's pursuit of Anne Boleyn. By 1529 Cromwell was one of Wolsey's most senior and trusted advisers.

Around 1528/9, Cromwell's wife Elizabeth and their daughters Anne and Grace all died, possibly due to an epidemic of 'sweating sickness'. Cromwell's will (see Chapter 4) was dated 12 July 1529 and provisions for his daughters were later crossed out.

1529

In October Wolsey was stripped of his government office and property over his failure to secure Henry's divorce. On 3 November 1529 Cromwell became member of parliament for Taunton, and was reported to be in favour with the king, despite his close connection with Wolsey.

1530

In November a warrant was drawn up for Wolsey's arrest on the grounds of treason for his conspiring against Anne Boleyn, but his ill health led to his death in Leicester on his journey (see Cavendish, Chapter 18). Before the year was over, Cromwell was made a member of the Privy Council, becoming a legal advisor to the king.

1531

In January Cromwell became a junior member of the King's Council. By the autumn he was supervising the king's legal and parliamentary affairs in conjunction with Thomas Audley.

1532

Sir Thomas More resigned as Lord Chancellor in May after his failure to preserve Henry's marriage to Catherine of Aragon. He was succeeded by Audley, which helped to cement Cromwell's influence at court. The king granted Cromwell the lordship of Romney in Newport, Wales. Cromwell was also made joint Master of the King's Jewel House in April, Clerk of the Hanaper [Hamper] in July and Master of the Court of Wards, plus appointed Receiver General and supervisor of the lands Wolsey had secured for Cardinal College in Oxford.

1533

On 26 January, Audley was appointed Lord Chancellor. Henry and Anne Boleyn married on 25 January 1533, after a secret marriage on 14 November 1532, probably in Calais. On 4 February, Cromwell introduced a new bill to parliament, restricting the right to make appeals to Rome. On 30 March, Thomas Cranmer was consecrated Archbishop of Canterbury. Cromwell's bill was passed into law in April as the Act in Restraint of Appeals, ensuring there could be no challenge to Henry's new marriage from Rome. Cranmer declared Henry's previous marriage illegal in May.

On 12 April Cromwell was appointed Chancellor of the Exchequer. In this year he was also made Recorder of Bristol and joint Steward of Westminster Abbey, plus joint Surveyor of the King's Woods.

In December, the King authorised Cromwell to discredit the Pope, who was widely attacked in sermons and pamphlets.

1534

A new Parliament was summoned, again under Cromwell's supervision, to enact the legislation needed to make a formal break of remaining ties with Rome. In April 1534, Henry confirmed Cromwell as his principal secretary and chief minister. Cromwell took prompt steps to enforce the new legislation: members of the Commons and the Lords were required to swear an oath accepting the Act of Succession, and all the king's subjects were now required to swear to the legitimacy of his new marriage and, by implication, the break from Rome. Thomas More refused and was sent to the Tower of London (he was executed in 1535).

When Parliament reconvened in November, Cromwell brought in significant new laws making it treasonous to speak rebellious words against the Royal Family, to deny their titles, or to call the king a heretic, tyrant, infidel or usurper. The Act of Supremacy also clarified the king's position as head of the church and the Act for Payment of First Fruits and Tenths substantially increased clerical taxes.

In this year Cromwell's other appointments included: Commissioner for the Subsidy, Kent; Master of the Rolls (from 8 October 1534 until 10 July 1536); joint Constable with his nephew Richard Williams (alias Cromwell) of Hertford Castle; Keeper of Berkeley Park and joint

Constable of Berkeley Castle; Master of the Game, and Keeper of Hynton Wood and Red Wood.

1535

On 21 January, the king appointed Cromwell Royal Vicegerent and Vicar-General, plus Visitor General of Religious Houses, and commissioned him to organise visitations of all the churches, monasteries and clergy in the country – he also organised destructive visitations to universities and colleges with strong church links, described by historian John Lawson as 'easily the greatest single disaster in English literary history'.

Cromwell's other appointments in 1535 included: Lordships of Edmonton and Sayesbery, Middlesex, and Leeds Castle, Kent; Steward of the Duchy of Lancaster for Essex, Hertfordshire and Middlesex; Steward of Savoy Manor; Chancellor, High Steward and Visitor, Cambridge University; Commissioner for the Peace in Bristol, Kent, Middlesex and Surrey; Bailiff of Enfield.

Cromwell is also believed to have had an illegitimate daughter, Jane, around this time. Her mother and details of her early life are unknown, but there are some records of her in Cheshire archives (she later married the son of Cromwell's agent in that region); she was living with Cromwell's son Gregory at Leeds Castle in 1539, and Cromwell paid for her expenses. Jane and her own family apparently remained staunch Roman Catholics; she died in 1580.

1536

Cromwell's latest Reformation legislation, an Act for the Suppression of the Lesser Monasterie (those with a gross income of less than £200 per annum) led to a disagreement with Anne Boleyn, formerly an ally, who wanted the proceeds to be used for education and charitable purposes rather than going to the king. On 2 April her almoner, John Skypp [or Skip, later Bishop of Hereford] gave an excoriating sermon clearly directed at Cromwell, urging 'that a King's councillor ought to take good heed what advice he gave in altering ancient things'. By now Henry was losing interest in Anne, in favour of Jane Seymour, and Cromwell was allegedly closely involved with accusations that Anne had committed adultery (see Chapters 8 and 16). Anne was executed on 19 May.

Cromwell succeeded Anne father, Thomas Boleyn, as Lord Privy Seal on 2 July, resigning the office of Master of the Rolls. Six days later he was raised to the peerage as Baron Cromwell of Okeham. In this year efforts were made to clarify religious doctrine after the break with Rome in the form of the Ten Articles, and Cromwell circulated injunctions for their enforcement; this provoked the uprising in northern England known as the Pilgrimage of Grace (see Chapter 16). One of the leaders, Thomas Darcy, prophetically observed to Cromwell on his own way to the gallows: 'It is thou that art the very original and chief causer of this rebellion and mischief, and art likewise causer of the apprehension of us that be noble men and dost daily earnestly travail to bring us our end and to strike off our heads, and I trust that or thou die, though thou wouldst procure all the noblemen's heads within the realm to be stricken off, yet shall there one head remain that shall strike off thy head.'

Cromwell's other new appointments in 1536 included: Lordship of the Manor of Writtle, Essex; Commissioner for the Peace for Essex; Prebendary of Salisbury; Receiver of Petitions in the Lords; and Prebendary of Blewbery, Salisbury; and he was knighted.

1537

In February 1537, Cromwell convened a synod, co-ordinated by Thomas Cranmer and Edward Foxe (Bishop of Hereford), and they prepared a draft document known as the Bishops' Book, an ancestor f the Thirty-Nine Articles of the Church of England published in 1571. Cromwell's influence, however, was weakened by the emergence of the Privy Council dominated by his conservative opponents. Cromwell was nonetheless appointed to the Order of the Garter on 5 August.

His other appointments in this year included: Lordship of Havering-atte-Bower, Essex; Commissioner for the Peace for Derbyshire and Westmorland; Dean of Wells; Warden and Chief Justice of the Royal Forests in Eyre, North of Trent.

Henry's third wife, Jane Seymour, died on 24 October; in August Cromwell's son Gregory had married her sister, Elizabeth.

1538

In January 1538, Cromwell pursued a campaign against 'idolatry' by the followers of Rome. Statues, rood screens, and images were attacked, culminating in September with the dismantling of the shrine of St Thomas Becket at Canterbury. He also condemned 'pilgrimages, feigned relics or images, or any such superstitions' and commanded: 'Ye shall provide one book of the whole Bible in English and set up the same in some convenient place within the said church...' (see Chapter 10).

In May a deputation from Germany arrived, with Cromwell interested in a Protestant alliance; during this visit he was told about the Duke of Cleves' two daughters.

Cromwell took the initiative against his enemies, imprisoning the Marquess of Exeter, Sir Edward Neville, and Sir Nicholas Carew on charges of treason in November, using evidence acquired by interrogation in the Tower. Some historians have suggested that the 'Exeter Conspiracy' to overthrow the king was exaggerated by Cromwell.

On 17 December 1538, the Inquisitor-General of France forbade the printing of Miles Coverdale's Great Bible. Cromwell persuaded the King of France to release the unfinished books so that printing could continue in England – it became available in April 1539.

Cromwell's appointments in 1538 included: Commissioner for the Peace, all counties; Steward, Surveyor, Receiver, and Bailiff of the Crown Lands of the Isle of Wight; Constable of Carisbrooke Castle.

1539

With resistance to the wide scope of the English Reformation growing, Thomas Howard, Duke of Norfolk (and Anne Boleyn's uncle)
drew up what became the Six Articles, reaffirming the role of mass,
the sacraments and the priesthood in worship. Norfolk and Cromwell
openly argued in front of the king and Archbishop Cranmer in June.

In October 1539, the King agreed to Cromwell's suggestion that he
should marry Anne of Cleves, partly influenced by Hans Holbein's
portrait of her. (Holbein also painted Cromwell (see Chapter 5), and
was to lose favour in the court after Cromwell's fall.) Anne, described
by the French ambassador Charles de Marillac as 'of middling beauty
and of very assured and resolute countenance', came to England in
December.

Cromwell's appointments in 1539 included: Commissioner for
Printing of the Bible; Commissioner for the Sale of Crown Lands;
Steward and Bailiff of Rayleigh and Rochford, Essex September;
Constable of Leeds Castle, Kent; High Steward of Reading.

1540

Henry met Anne of Cleves for the first time in January, at Rochester,
and declared he did not like her, though went ahead with the
marriage. Despite Henry's displeasure, on 18 April he granted
Cromwell the earldom of Essex, as well as making him Lord Great
Chamberlain in his court; he was also appointed Steward of the
Monastery of Furness in this year.

The Duke of Norfolk and the Bishop of Winchester, Stephen
Gardiner, seized their opportunity to move against Cromwell.
Howard placed another niece of his, Catherine Howard, in the court
as a lady-in-waiting, and she caught Henry's eye as intended. Meanwhile Cromwell was arrested at a Council meeting on 10 June and
imprisoned in the Tower of London. A Bill of Attainder was drawn up
listing his crimes, including corruption, acting for personal gain and
heresy, as well as allegedly plotting to marry Henry's daughter Mary

Tudor (later Mary I); it was passed into law on 29 June, and Cromwell was stripped of many of his honours, although his son was allowed to inherit the title of Baron Cromwell in December. The bill declared that he was 'a man of very base and low degree' and that he should thereafter only be known as 'Thomas Cromwell, cloth carder'.

He was condemned to death without trial and was beheaded in public at Tower Hill on 28 July – Henry meanwhile married Catherine Howard on the same day. There are various accounts of the execution, some suggesting the executioner had difficulty severing his head, but the precise circumstances are uncertain. His head was set on a spike on London Bridge.

1

SPEECH BY CROMWELL (APRIL 1523)

Cromwell is generally believed to have been the author of this speech, recorded in state papers, for a debate about invasion of France, although it is not known if he actually delivered it. Henry VIII had declared war against France (and its ally Scotland) and Wolsey had asked for funds to support Henry's invasion in person. Cromwell manages to combine support for the king with his own view that this was not a good proposal, and that the focus should be on subjugating Scotland.

It is no time now to speak of peace. Want of truth is so deeply rooted in the French nation, and their appetite to extend their bounds is so insatiable, that even if we had no quarrel of our own against them, we could not but detest their false dealings with other princes. If not scourged, they will be a scourge to others. They have provoked the Emperor, whose power is so great that, when it is joined with ours, they will be environed on every side. The Emperor has already shown them what he can do, by recovering Navarre, the city of Tournay and the Tournesis, and has driven them quite out of Italy, dispossessing them of the noble duchy of Milan, the getting and defending of which was so expensive to them and Genoa; and we, for our part, have spoiled and burnt Morkesse, and laid waste a great country, with great honour to the fortunate and sage captain, the earl of Surrey, who remained in the French dominions, with a small number of men, for six or seven weeks, when all the power of France durst not give him battle. I trust the same valiant captain will subdue the Scots, whom the French have so 'custuously' entertained against us. It may be a question whether to continue the same kind of war as hitherto, or to make it more sharp and violent by sending such a force as utterly to subdue Francis. On this point I wish some sage and experienced person would speak; only one thing 'putteth me in no small agony.' My lord Cardinal said that the King, who is dearer to any of his subjects than his own life, intends to go over in person; which I wish I may never live to see. 'I am sure there is no good Englishman which can be merry the day when he happeneth to think that his grace might perchance be distempered of his health; so that, albeit I say for my part, I stomach, as a sorry subject may do, the high injuries done by the said Françoys unto his most dear sovereign, yet, rather than the thing should go so far forth, I could, for my part, be contented to forget altogether.'

The French have established an ordinance among them, that their King shall never go in person, in ranged battle, against our nation, on account of the danger, notwithstanding their marvellous policy for the sure succession of their crown. How needful, then, for us '(considering in what case we be)' to entreat our sovereign, for our sakes and his daughter's, 'upon whose weal and circumspect bestowing, next his noble person, dependeth all our wealths,' to restrain his high courage; for, if he were to go, I am sure there would not be one man in the army 'but he should be more meet to wail and wring his hands, than assured to fight, when he considered that, if otherwise than well should fortune to that precious jewel, which he had for his party in custody, it were more meeter for him to depart into Turkey, than to return again into his natural country to his wife and children.' I think, therefore, if my prince would tarry within his realm, it would be better to advance our war by little and little, so as to weary out the said Françoys, than send over at once the power royal of the kingdom.

'In the reasoning of which matter I shall but utter mine ignorance afore Hannibal, as our right wise speaker rehearsed now of late;' but having gone thus far, I shall utter my poor mind, if this great army of 30,000 foot and 10,000 horse should be conveyed beyond sea, what way they may most annoy our enemies with the greatest safety, and how they may be victualled. If they could be victualled out of the archdukedom, I doubt not they would return in safety; for as their enemies did not venture last year to attack the earl of Surrey, they would all the more beware of so great an army; but by this means the harm they would do to France would not be so great as what we ourselves should sustain in supporting such a force. Before three summers were over, the army would exhaust all the coin and bullion in the realm, which I conjecture cannot much exceed a million; for if the value of the whole realm exceed not four millions, as my lord Cardinal told us plainly, 'of which the possessions were esteemed to amount to one whole million,' there can be no doubt that the corn, cattle, commodities and utensils, and apparel for men and women, which was never so sumptuous, and the wares, made not only from our own produce, but from the parts beyond sea, of which there was never so great abundance, amount at least to other two millions. Thus we should soon be made incapable of helping or hurting any one, and be compelled, as we once did, to coin leather. This, for my part, I could be content with; but if the King will go over in person, and should happen to fall into the hands of the enemy, which God forbid, how should we be able to redeem him? 'If they will nought for their wines but gold, they would think great scorn to take leather for our prince.'

And of the inhabitants of the archdukedom, how desirous they are to have much of our money for little of their victuals, we had good experience, when the King last went over, and last year, when my lord of Surrey was sent. But if we must send the army through their possessions, and go direct to Paris, which no doubt may be easily got, as soon as we have left the marches of the archdukedom, we should be on our guard against the Frenchmen's mode of fighting, whose plan is, not to meddle with our army, but lie in wait for stragglers or conductors of victuals. We shall be sure to find no victuals in our way, and might find the danger of leaving strongholds behind us, which the politic prince, Henry VII., avoided; for when he crossed the sea, he laid siege to Boulogne before he would enter any further into France; and the present King, when he purposed, as I have been told, to go to Paris, began at Terouenne, 'and the Emperor employed whosoever be in Tournay,' not thinking it right to pass further, leaving strongholds behind him in the possession of the enemy. What expense it would be, thus to employ our army, the King has had too good experience, in the winning of Terouenne, which cost him more than twenty such ungracious dogholes could be worth. But, if instead of this, we invaded Normandy, Brittany or some province on the sea, I can see nothing but danger on every side, not only at their arrival among their enemies, but from the difficulty in victualling them while they remain there; for though we are undoubtedly much diminished in treasure, we have a far greater want of defensible men. If I am asked why I urge these objections, I think the advantages we have had over the French have put them in despair to try it with us any more in ranged battle; but the French know as well our impatience to continue in war many years, especially in winter, as that our nation is invincible in arms.

I will now show you the advantages former kings have had over us in making war against France. In former times we had always places where we could land in security, either of our own, or of our confederates, in Gascony, Guienne, Brittany or Normandy. The towns and strongholds were of nothing like the strength they are at present. What friends we have now, I dare not venture to speak, and no nation was ever so united as our enemy. While the Emperor was here, occupied with the winning of Tournay, they corrupted three or four of the greatest nobles of Spain, on whom the Emperor was compelled to do justice on his return thither. Even my lord of Chievres, who was most bound to the Emperor, I heard my lord Cardinal say, was corrupted by their policy and gifts; and since his majesty's return to Spain, the governors of his archdukedom have granted safe conducts to French and Scotch merchants; which is a marvellous hindrance, for if our commodities had been as well kept from them as theirs from us,

many a thousand French artificers, who have no living but by
working our wools, would have been compelled to cry to the King for
peace. The King should devote all his efforts to the subjugation of
Scotland, and to join that realm to his, so that both they and we might
live under one obeisance, law and policy, for ever. This would secure
him the highest honour any king of England has reached, and it
would be the greatest abashment to Francis. And though it be a
common saying, that in Scotland is nought to win but strokes, there is
another saying, 'who that intendeth France to win, with Scotland let
him begin.' It is mere folly to think of keeping possessions in France,
which is severed from us by the sea, while we allow Scotland,
belonging to the same island, to recognise another prince. This, once
united to England, all other possessions are easily retained.

2

LETTER FROM CROMWELL (AUGUST 1523)

Although much of Cromwell's official correspondence has survived in the Letters and Papers, Foreign and Domestic of Henry VIII, this letter is a rare example with a personal touch, sent to his friend Thomas Creke and demonstrating his conversational tone.

Supposing ye desire to know the news current in these parts, for it is said that news refresheth the spirit of life; wherefore ye shall understand that by long time I, amongst other, have indured a parliament, which continued by the space of 17 whole weeks, where we communed of war, peace, strife, contention, debate, murmur, grudge, riches, poverty, penury, truth, falsehood, justice, equity, deceit, oppression, magnanimity, activity, force, attempraunce, treason, murder, felony, consyl[ment?], and also how [the words 'to devise' have been struck out here] a commonwealth might be edified and a[lso] continued within our realm. Howbeit, in conclusion, we have do[ne] as our predecessors have been wont to do, that is to say, as well as we might, and left where we began. Ye shall also understand the duke of Suffolk, furnished with a great army, goeth over in all goodly haste, [whit]her I know not; when I know I shall advertise you. We have in our parliament granted unto the King's highness a right large subsidy, the like whereof was never granted in this realm.

All your friends to my knowledge be in good health, and specially they that ye wot of; ye know what I mean. I think it best to write in parables, because I am in doubt. Master Vawhan [Vaughan] fareth well, and so doth Master Munkcaster. Master Woodall is merry without a wife, and commendeth him to you; and so is also Nicholas Longmede, which hath paid William Wilforde.

3

LETTER FROM CROMWELL (NOVEMBER 1525)

(A rare personal letter sent to his wife.)

Elyzabeth I commend me unto you and have sente you by this berer a fatt doo [doe], the one half whereof I pray you may be delyvered unto my gossyp mastres Smyth, and with the rest to use your pleasure. And further yf Richard Swifte be cum home or fortune to cum shortly, I will that he resorte to me at Begham or Tonbridge with all dylygence. Such news as ye have in those partyes I pray you sende me parte by this berer. At Begham the xxixth day of November. And farther I pray you sende me word in wryting who hathe resorted unto you syns my departuer from you to speke with me.

Per your husbend

Thomas Crumwell.

Add. To my well beloved wyf Elyzabeth Crumwell agenst the Freyers Augustines in London be this given.

4

CROMWELL'S WILL (1529)

(The italic sections in square brackets were later removed – some due to the early death of his daughters.)

In the name of God, Amen. The 12th day of July, in the year of our Lord God MCCCCCXXIX., and in the 21st year of the reign of our Sovereign Lord, King Henry VIII., I, Thomas Cromwell, of London, Gentleman, being whole in body and in good and perfect memory, lauded be the Holy Trinity, make, ordain, and declare this my present testament, containing my last will, in manner as following:—First I bequeath my soul to the great God of heaven, my Maker, Creator, and Redeemer, beseeching the most glorious Virgin and blessed Lady Saint Mary the Virgin and Mother, with all the holy company of heaven, to be mediators and intercessors for me to the Holy Trinity, so that I may be able, when it shall please Almighty God to call me out of this miserable world and transitory life, to inherit the kingdom of heaven amongst the number of good Christian people; and whensoever I shall depart this present life I bequeath my body to be buried where it shall please God to ordain me to die, and to be ordered after the discretion of mine executors undernamed. And for my goods which our Lord hath lent me in this world, I will shall be ordered and disposed in manner and form as hereafter shall ensue. First I give and bequeath unto my son Gregory Cromwell six hundred threescore six pounds, thirteen shillings, and fourpence, of lawful money of England, with the which six hundred threescore six pounds, thirteen shillings, and fourpence, I will mine executors undernamed immediately or as soon as they conveniently may after my decease, shall purchase lands, tenements, and hereditaments to the clear yearly value of £33 6s. 8d. by the year above all charges and reprises to the use of my said son Gregory, for term of his life; and after the decease of the said Gregory to the heirs male of his body lawfully to be begotten, and for lack of heirs male of the body of the said Gregory, lawfully begotten, to the heirs general of his body lawfully begotten. And for lack of such heirs to the right heirs of me the said Thomas Cromwell, in fee. I will also that immediately and as soon as the said lands, tenements, and hereditaments shall be so purchased after my death as is aforesaid by mine executors, that the yearly profits thereof shall be wholly spent and employed in and about the education and finding honestly of my said son Gregory, in virtue, good learning, and manners, until such time as he shall come to the full age of 24 years. During which time I heartily desire and require my said executors to be good unto my said you Gregory, and to see he do lose no time, but to see him virtuously ordered and brought up according to my trust.

Item. I give and bequeath to my said son Gregory, (when he shall come to his full age of 24 years), two hundred pounds of lawful English money to order them as our Lord shall give him grace and discretion, which £200 I will shall be put in surety to the intent the same may come to his hands at his said age of 24 years.

Item. I give and bequeath to my said son Gregory of such household stuff as God hath lent me, three of my best featherbeds with their bolsters; and, the best pair of blankets of fustian, my best coverlet of tapestry, and my quilt of yellow Turkey satin; one pair of my best sheets, four pillows of down, with four pair of the best pillowberes, four of my best table-cloths, four of my best towels, two dozen of my finest napkins, and two dozen of my other napkins, two garnish of my best vessel, three of my best brass pots, three of my best brass pans, two of my best kettles, two of my best spits, my best joined bed of Flanders work, with the best —— and tester, and other the appurtenances thereto belonging; my best press, carven of Flanders work, and my best cupboard, carven of Flanders work, with also six joined stools of Flanders work, and six of my best cushions.

Item. I give and bequeath to my said son Gregory a basin with an ewer parcel-gilt, my best salt gilt, my best cup gilt, three of my best goblets; three other of my goblets parcel-gilt, twelve of my best silver spoons, three of my best drinking ale-pots gilt; all the which parcels of plate and household stuff I will shall be safely kept to the use of my said you Gregory till he shall come to his said full age of 24. And all the which plate, household stuff, napery, and all other the premises, I will mine executors do put in safe keeping until my said son come to the said years or age of 24. And if he die before the age of 24, then I will all the said plate, vessel, and household stuff shall be sold by mine executors. And the money thereof coming to be given and equally divided amongst my poor kinsfolk, that is to say, amongst the children as well of mine own sisters Elizabeth and Katherine, as of my late wife's sister Joan, wife to John Williamson; and if it happen that all the children of my said sisters and sister-in-law do die before the partition be made, and none of them be living, then I will that all the said plate, vessel, and household stuff shall be sold and given to other my poor kinsfolk then being in life, and other poor and indigent people, in deeds of charity for my soul, my father and mother their souls, and all Christian souls.

[Item. I give and bequeath to my daughter Anne an hundred marks of lawful money of England when she shall come to her lawful age or happen to be married, and £40 toward her finding until the time that she shall be of lawful age or be married, which £40 I will shall be delivered to my friend John Cook, one of the six Clerks of the King's Chancery, to the intent he may order the same and cause the same to be employed in the best wise he can devise about the virtuous education and bringing up of my said daughter till she shall come to her lawful age or marriage. Then I will that the said 100 marks, and so much of the said £40 as then shall be unspent and unemployed at the day of the death of my said daughter Anne, I will it shall

remain to Gregory my son, if he then be in life; and if he be dead, the same
hundred marks, and also so much of the said £40 as then shall be unspent,
to be departed amongst my sisters' children, in manner and form aforesaid.
And if it happen my said sisters' children then to be all dead, then I will the
said 100 marks and so much of the said £40 as shall be unspent, shall be
divided amongst my kinsfolk, such as then, shall be in life.]

Item. I give and bequeath unto my sister Elizabeth Wellyfed £40,
three goblets without a cover, a mazer, and a nut.

Item. I give and bequeath to my nephew Richard Willyams *[ser-*
vant with my Lord Marquess Dorset, £66 13s. 4d.], £40 sterling, my
~~fourth~~ best gown, doublet, and jacket.

Item. I give and bequeath to my nephew, Christopher Wellyfed
£40, *[£20]* my fifth gown, doublet, and jacket.

Item. I give and bequeath to my nephew William Wellyfed the
younger £20, *[£40]*.

Item. I give and bequeath to my niece Alice Wellyfed, to her
marriage, £20. And if it happen her to die before marriage, then I will
that the said £20 shall remain to her brother Christopher. And if it
happen him to die, the same £20 to remain to Wm. Wellyfed the
younger, his brother. And if it happen them all to die before their
lawful age or marriage, then I will that all their parts shall remain to
Gregory my son. And if it happen him to die before them, then I will
all the said parts shall remain *[to Anne and Grace, my daughters]* to
Richard Willyams and Walter Willyams, my nephews. And if it
happen them to die, then I will that all the said parts shall be
distributed in deeds of charity for my soul, my father's and mother's
souls, and all Christian souls.

Item. I give and bequeath to my mother-in-law Mercy Prior, £40
of lawful English money, and her chamber, with certain household
stuff; that is to say, a featherbed, a bolster, two pillows with their
beres, six pair of sheets, a pair of blankets, a garnish of vessel, two
pots, two pans, two spits, with such other of my household stuff as
shall be thought meet for her by the discretion of mine executors,
and such as she will reasonably desire, not being bequeathed to other
uses in this my present testament and last will.

Item. I give and bequeath to my said mother-in-law a little salt of silver, a mazer, six silver spoons, and a drinking-pot of silver. And also I charge mine executors to be good unto her during her life.

Item. I give and bequeath to my brother-in-law William Wellyfed, £20, my third gown, jacket, and doublet.

Item. I give and bequeath to John Willyams my brother-in-law, 100 marks, a gown, a doublet, a jacket, a featherbed, a bolster, six pair of sheets, two table-cloths, two dozen napkins, two towels, two brass pots, two brass pans, a silver pot, a nut parcel-gilt; and to Joan, his wife, £40.

Item. I give and bequeath to Joan Willyams, their daughter, to her marriage, £20, and to every other of their children, £12 13s. 4d.

Item. I bequeath to Walter Willyams, my nephew, £20.

Item. I give and bequeath to Ralph Sadler, my servant, 200 marks of lawful English money, my second gown, jacket, and doublet, and all my books.

Item. I give and bequeath to Hugh Whalley, my servant, £6 13s. 4d.

Item. I give and bequeath to Stephen Vaughan, sometime my servant, 100 marks, a gown, jacket, and doublet.

Item. I give and bequeath to Page, my servant, otherwise called John De Fount, £6 13s. 4d.

[Item. I give and bequeath to Elizabeth Gregory, sometime my servant, £20, six pair of sheets, a featherbed, a pair of blankets, a coverlet, two table-cloths, one dozen napkins, two brass pots, two pans, two spits.] And also to Thomas Averey, my servant, £6 13s.4d.

[Item. I give and bequeath to John Cooke, one of the six Master Clerks of the Chancery, £10, my second gown, doublet, and jacket.

Item. I give and bequeath to Roger More, servant of the King's bake-house, £6 13s. 4d., three yards of satin; and to Maudelyn, his wife, £3 6s. 8d.]

Item. I give and bequeath to John Horwood, £6 13s. 4d.

[Item. I give and bequeath to my little daughter Grace 100 marks of lawful English money when she shall come to her lawful age or marriage; and also £40 towards her exhibition and finding until such time she shall be of lawful age or be married, which £40 I will shall be delivered to my brother-in-law, John Willyams, to the intent he may order and cause the *same to be employed in and about the virtuous education and bringing up of my said daughter, till she shall come to her lawful age of marriage. And if it happen my said daughter to die before she come to her lawful age or marriage, then I will that the said 100 marks, and so much of the said £40 as shall then be unspent and unemployed about the finding of my said daughter at the day of the death of my said daughter shall remain and be delivered to Gregory my son, if he then shall happen to be in life; and if he be dead, then the said 100 marks, and the said residue of the said £40, to be evenly departed among my grown kinsfolk—that is to say, my sisters' children aforesaid.]*

Item. That the rest of mine apparel before not given or bequeathed in this my testament and last will shall be given and equally departed amongst my servants after the order and discretion of mine executors.

Item. I will also that mine executors shall take the yearly profits above the charges of my farm of Carberry, and all other things contained in my said lease of Carberry, in the county of Middlesex, and with the profits thereof shall yearly pay unto my brother-in-law William [Wellyfed] and Elizabeth his wife, mine only sister, twenty pounds; give and distribute for my soul quarterly 40 shillings during their lives and the longer of them; and after the decease of the said William and Elizabeth, the profits of the said farm over and above the yearly rent to be kept to the use of my son Gregory till he be come to the age of 24 years. And at the years of 24 the said lease and farm of Carberry, I do give and bequeath to my son Gregory, to have the same to him, his executors and assigns. And if it fortune the said Gregory my son to die before, my said brother-in-law and sister being dead, he shall come to the age of 24 years, then I will my said cousin Richard Willyams shall have the farm with the appurtenances to him and to his executors and assigns; and if it happen my said brother-in-law, my sister, my son Gregory, and my said cousin Richard, to die before the accomplishment of this my will touching the said farm, then I will mine executors shall sell the said farm, and the money thereof coming to employ in deeds of charity, to pray for my soul and all Christian souls.

Item. I will mine executors shall conduct and hire a priest, being an honest person of continent and good living, to sing for my soul by the space of seven years next after my death, and to give him for the same £6 13s. 4d. for his stipend.

Item. I give and bequeath towards the making of highways in this realm, where it shall be thought most necessary, £20 to be disposed by the discretion of mine executors.

Item. I give and bequeath to every the five orders of Friars within the City of London, to pray for my soul, 20 shillings.

Item. I give and bequeath to 60 poor maidens in marriage, £40, that is to say, 13s. 4d. to every of the said poor maidens, to be given and distributed by the discretion of mine executors.

Item. I will that there shall be dealt and given after my decease amongst poor people householders, to pray for my soul, £20, such as by mine executors shall be thought most needful.

Item. I give and bequeath to the poor parishioners of the parish where God shall ordain me to have my dwellingplace at the time of my death, £10, to be truly distributed amongst them by the discretion of mine executors.

Item. I give and bequeath to my parish church for my tithes forgotten, 20 shillings.

Item. To the poor prisoners of Newgate, Ludgate, King's Bench, and Marshalsea, to be equally distributed amongst them, £10. Willing, charging, and desiring mine executors underwritten, that they shall see this my will performed in every point according to my true meaning and intent as they will answer to God, and discharge their consciences. The residue of all my goods, chattels, and debts not bequeathed, my funeral and burial performed, which I will shall be done without any earthly pomp, and my debts paid, I will shall be sold, and the money thereof coming, to be distributed in works of charity and pity, after the good discretion of mine executors under-named. Whom I make and ordain, Stephen Vaughan, Ralph Sadler, my servants, and John Willyams my brother-in-law. Praying and desiring the same mine executors to be good unto my son Gregory, and to all other my poor friends and kinsfolk and servants aforenamed in this my testament. And of this my present testament and last will I make Roger More mine overseer; unto whom and also to every of the other mine executors I give and bequeath £6 13s. 4d. for their pains to be taken in the execution of this my last will and testament, over and above such legacies as herebefore I have bequeathed them in this same testament and will. In witness whereof, to this my present testament and last will I have set to my hand in every leaf contained in this book, the day and year before limited.

Item. I give and bequeath to William Brabazon, my servant, £20 8s., a gun, a doublet, a jacket, and my second gelding.

It. to John Avery, Yeoman of the Bedchamber with the King's Highness, £6 13s. 4d., and a doublet of satin.

It. to Thurston, my cook. £6 13s. 4d.

It. to William Body, my servant, £6 13s. 4d.

It. to Peter Mewtas, my servant, £6 13s. 4d.

It. to Ric. Sleysh, my servant, £6 13s. 4d.

It. to George Wilkinson, my servant, £6 13s. 4d.

It. to my friend, Thomas Alvard. £10, and my best gelding.

It. to my friend, Thomas Rush, £10.

It. to my servant, John Hynde, my horsekeeper, £3 6s. 8d.

Item. I will that mine executors shall safely keep the patent of the manor of Romney to the use of my son Gregory, and the money growing thereof, till he shall come to his lawful age, to be yearly received to the use of my said son, and the whole revenue thereof coming to be truly paid unto him at such time as he shall come to the age of 24 years.

per me Thomam Crumwell

5

HOLBEIN'S PORTRAIT (C.1532)

Hans Holbein the Younger (c.1497–1543) was a German painter and printmaker regarded as one of the great portraitists of the 16th century. In 1526 he went to England looking for work, and was embraced in Thomas More's circle; he then returned in 1532, with Anne Boleyn and Cromwell as his patrons. By 1535 he was the king's official painter, although he later fell out of favour, aided by Cromwell's disgrace and the king's belief that Holbein's portrait of Anne of Cleves overstated her beauty.

His portrait of Cromwell, on the cover of this book, is the only one known of Cromwell in his lifetime (though it survives in three versions, all copies of the original), and spawned many imitations in subsequent centuries.

The inscription on the border reads: 'To our trusty and right well, beloved Councillor, Thomas Cromwell, Master of our Jewel House.' Cromwell sits holding a legal document, with objects in front of him including a quill, a devotional book, scissors and a leather bag.

6

WRIOTHESLEY'S CHRONICLE (1534-40)

Charles Wriothesley (1508–1562) was a herald at the College of Arms in London. He attended Anne Boleyn's coronation in 1533. His *A Chronicle of England During the Reigns of the Tudors, From A.D. 1485 to 1559*, usually known as *Wriothesley's Chronicle*, was written as diaries during the reigns of Henry VIII and his three children who succeeded him, and only published in 1875.

1534

This yeare allso, in the beginninge of Michaellmasse terme, Mr. Thomas Crumwell was made Master of the Rolles, and tooke his oathe in the Chauncerie the first day of the same terme. [Cromwell was made Master of the Rolls on 8 October.]

1535

Also this yeare Mr. Thomas Cromwell and Doctor [Thomas] Lee visited all the religious places in Englande, being ordayned by the Kinges grace for his high visitors, and they tooke out of everie religious house all religious persons from the age of 24 years and under, and shewed them how they shoulde use wilfull povertie, and also he closed up all the residue of the religious persons booth men and weomen that would Remaine still, so that they should not come out of their places, nor no men resorte to the places of nonnes [nuns], nor weomen to come into the places of religious men, but onelie to heere service and masses in their churches, and also they tooke out of divers churches of England certaine reliques that the people were wont to worshipp, as Our Ladies girdell at Westminster, which weomen with chield were wont to girde with, and Sainct Elizabethes girdell, and in Poules a relique of Our Ladies milke, which was broken and founde but a peece of chalke, with other reliques in divers places which they used for covetousnes in deceaphing the people. [Cromwell was chosen to manage this inquiry under the name of Visitor-General; Thomas Lee was one of his deputies.]

1536

And the seconde daie of Maie, Mr. Norris and my Lorde of Rochforde were brought to the Towre of London as prisonners; Queen Anne and the same daie, about five of the clocke at night, the Queene Tower. Anne Bolleine was brought to the Towre of London by my Lord Chauncelor, the Duke of Norfolke, Mr. Secretarie [i.e. Cromwell], and Sir William Kingston, Constable of the Tower ; and when she came to the court gate, entring in, she fell downe on her knees before the said lordes, beseeching God to helpe her as she was not giltie of her accusement, and also desired the said lordes to beseech the Kinges grace to be good unto her, and so they left her their prisoner.

Item, this yeare, in Trinitie terme, the Soundaie after Corpus Christi daie [i.e. on 18 June], the Erle of Wilshire, Sir Thomas Bolleine, father to Queene Anne, delivered the Kinges Privie Seale, wherof he was Custos, into the Kinges handes; and after Sainct Peeters daie, at Midsommer, Mr. Thomas Crumwell, Secretarie to the Kinges Grace and Master of the Rolls, had the Privie Seale delivered to him, to be Lorde and Custos therof...

This yeare, on Reliques Soundaye, beinge the 9 daye of Julye, the Lord Fyzt-Waren was created Erle of Bathe at Yorke Place by Westmynster, and the morrowe after Mr. Thomas Cromwell was made Lord Cromewell by the Kinges letter patent under the Kinges brode seale...

Alsoe on Tuesdaye, the 18 daye of Julye, the Parlyament brake upp and was cleane dyssolved; at afternone the Kinge and all his lordes syttinge in there Parlyament robes, and alsoe the French Ambassadors were brought into the Parlyament Chamber to see the order and manner there, which the Kinges Grace himselfe dyd declare to the sayd Ambassadors in Frenche; also Mr. Thomas Cromewell, otherwise called Lord Crumwell, Lord Prevaye Seale, and Secretarye to the Kinge, was made Knight there in the Parliament Chamber, and one Mr. Pawlet also; also Mr. Secretorye, Lord Prevaye Seale, was made Highe Vycar over the Spiritualtye under the Kinge, and satt diverse tymes in the Convocation howse amonge the byshopps as headd over them. [i.e. Cromwell was made Vicar-General, sitting above the Archbishop of Canterbury]

Also, the twentith daie of Julie, the Convocation brooke upp at Poules and was dissolved, where the Lord Crumwell was present as the Kinges Vicar, and their caused all the bishopps, abbottes, and all other of the cleargie, being of the Convocation, to subscribe their names to an Act made their, which is this: That if the Kinges Grace or his deputie be cited at any tyme heareafter by the Emperoure or Bishopp of Rome to appeare at any Generall Counsell kept by them at any place whatsoeaver it shall be kept; that the King is not bounde to appeare, nor non other of this realme for him, because this realme is a whole monarchic and an emperiall sea of itself, and hath power to make lawes and reforme them booth concerning faith and all other lawes, the King heere and our Emperour being the onelie supream heade of the Holie Catholike Church of Englande next ymediatlie under God, and his clergie and Convocation of this realme are utterlie to disanull all the Bishopp of Romes auctoritie and lawes, saving fower Generall Councells which were kept at Mycenae [Nicaeum], &c., as by a booke of the same it shall appeare, which the whole cleargie of this realme as recognised the same.

Also, in the beginning of September, Sir Thomas Crumwell, Lord Crumwell, Keeper of the Privie Seale of our soveraigne lorde the Kinge, Vicegerent to the same of all his jurisdiction ecclesiasticall, visiting, by the Kinges supreame aucthoritie ecclesiasticall, the people and cleargie of this realme of Englande, sent out, under the Kinges Spirituall Seale, certaine Injunctions to the prelates and cleargie of this realme, for a good and vertuous order to be kept and had of the said cleargie, and declaring by the said Injunctions how the curates should preach and teatch their parishiones the 'Pater noster,' 'Avee,' and 'Creede,' the Commandementes of God, and the Articlees of the Faith in our maternall English tonge, with other certaine Injunctions for and concerning the vertuous living of the said cleargie, in geving good ensample to their parishioners, under a certaine paine lymitted for the same for the said cleargie that doe breake the same.

1537

This yeare, on Soundaie the 26th daie of August, the Lord Crumwell was made Knight of the Garter and stalled at Wyndsore.

1539

This yere the thirde daye of Maye the images at the Mounte besyde the Charterhouse were taken downe by my Lorde Privie Seales [i.e.

Cromwell's] commaundement because the people should use noe more idolatrye.

This yere the 8th daye of Maye, beinge Thursday, all the citizens of London mustered in harnes afore the Kinge; they gathered and assembled togither at Myles Ende and Stepney, and soe there were sett in aray in three battells, and so went in aray in at Algate and through Cornehill and Cheape to Westminster, and round about the Kinges parke at St. James, and soe over the feildes into Hoiborne and in at Newegate, and there brake of every man to his house...

My Lord Cromwell had amonge them one [1000] men of gunners, morris pykes, and bowemen, goeing in jerkins after the socheners [armed tenants] fashion, and his gentlemen goeinge by, to sett them in array, in jerkins of buffe leather, dublets and hose of white satten and taffata sarsenet, which he did for the honour of the citye; and Mr. Gregory Cromwell, and Mr. Richard Crumwell, with Sir Christofer Morris, Master of the Ordinance, and other of the Kinges servauntes, followed the ende of the last battell, rydinge on goodly horses and well apparayled.

[Gregory was Cromwell's son; Richard Williams was his nephew, and took the surname Cromwell/Cromwell; Richard was the great-grandfather of Oliver Cromwell. The event described is the 'Great London Muster', when Henry ordered a muster of all male subjects aged 16 to 60 in anticipation of possible invasion by the Catholics under Charles V. Around 16,500 men are said to have assembled.]

1540

This yeare, the 28th daie of Julie, Sir Thomas Crumwell, Earle of Essex, was beheaded at the Tower Hill, and Walter Lord named Hungerforde was beheaded with him, also for treason of boggery, their heades sett on London Bridge, and their bodies were buried within the Tower of London ; they were condemned by the whole bodie of this last Perliament, Thomas Cromwell for heresie, treason, and fellonie, and extortion.

LETTER FROM STARKEY (1535)

Thomas Starkey (c.1495–1538) was a political theorist who supported Cromwell, and published a defence of royal supremacy. This letter was written to Cromwell on 14 February 1535.

The communication I had with you when you delivered me this book, declaring how you had formed your judgment by long experience and deep considerations of God, of nature and of other politic and worldly things, has convinced me of your good opinion of me. Such wisdom I have found in few men who have given their lives to the study of letters, whereof you never have made any great profession. You have bound me to your service more by these gifts of your nature than by any worldly promotions, for I have never esteemed such things so highly as to make myself a slave to them. At our communication you spoke of some things 'whereof I have long fancied with myself,' and I will briefly give you my opinion of them...

LETTERS FROM CHAPUYS (1535–6)

Eustace Chapuys (c.1490/1556), was a diplomat from the Duchy of Savoy. He served the Holy Roman Emperor Charles V as imperial ambassador to England from 1529 until 1545. He is remembered for his extensive correspondence. He was a near neighbour of Cromwell in Austin Friars, London. In this short letter to Charles V's close advisor Nicolas de Granvelle (1486–1550), from 1535, he gives a contemporary account of Cromwell's origins.

As you desire me to give you a detailed account of secretary Cromwell and his origin, I will tell you that he is the son of a poor blacksmith, who lived and is buried at a small village distant one league and a half from this city (London). His uncle, the father of a cousin of his, whom he has since considerably enriched, was cook to the last archbishop of Canterbury [Warham]. In his youth Cromwell was rather ill-conditioned and wild. After being some time in prison he went to Flanders, Rome, and other places in Italy, where he made some stay. On his return to England he married the daughter of a fuller, and for a time kept servants in his house who worked for him at that handicraft. Later on he became a solicitor, and thereby became known to the late cardinal of York [Wolsey], who took him into his service. At his master's fall he behaved very well towards him; and on the Cardinal's death, Master Wallop, now ambassador at the Court of France, somehow threatened and insulted him; whereupon, to save himself, he [Cromwell] asked and obtained an audience from king Henry, whom he addressed in such flattering terms and eloquent language — promising to make him the richest King in the world — that the King at once took him into his service, and made him councillor, though his appointment was kept secret for more than four months. Since then he has been constantly rising in power, so much so that he has now more influence with his master than the Cardinal ever had; for in the latter's time there were Compton, the duke of Suffolk, and others, to whose advice the King occasionally listened, whereas nowadays everything is done at his bidding. The Chancellor [Audley] is but a tool in his hands.

Cromwell is eloquent in his own language, and, besides, speaks Latin, French, and Italian tolerably well. He lives splendidly; is very liberal both of money and fair words, and remarkably fond of pomp and ostentation in his household and in building.

In this letter to Charles V from 6 June 1536, Chapuys discusses Cromwell's role in Anne Boleyn's alleged adultery.

On the 24th inst., the eve of Ascension Day, immediately after the return of the express I sent to Your Majesty at Pontremoli, secretary Cromwell forwarded to me the packet of letters dated from that town, desiring me at the same time to inform him as soon as possible of their contents. For the last two days, said the message, he (Cromwell) had fully intended to call on me according to promise, but had been prevented by press of business; he would, however, do so as soon as disengaged. Hearing which, I did not hesitate, and in order the more to oblige him and dispose him to attend to my requests, determined to repair to his hotel, which I did shortly after. On my arrival there Cromwell told me how he had on that very morning repaired to

Court, and seen the King for the sole and express purpose of obtaining an audience for me, and that the King had willingly granted me one for the day after the arrival of the courier, who, he said, had brought despatches from the King's ambassador at Your Majesty's court, so full of pleasant news and assurances of your sincere good-will that nothing more could be desired. Cromwell further assured me that he was more happy and content at that than if he had gained at play 100,000 livres at a single stroke. He had not the least doubt that I should find the King much better disposed than he had hitherto been, not only with regard to the principal matters under discussion, but likewise in reference to my own particular affairs; for, said he, 'the King's affectionate love for you has lately been on the increase, owing to certain letters you have lately addressed (the copy of which I now forward) to Mr. de Granvelle. Now-a-days, Cromwell observed, since the execution of the Royal mistress, things will go on better than before, as you may well consider.'

He himself had been authorised and commissioned by the King to prosecute and bring to an end the mistress's trial, to do which he had taken considerable trouble. It was he who, in consequence of the disappointment and anger he had felt on hearing the King's answer to me on the third day of Easter, had planned and brought about the whole affair.

One of the things which had mostly raised his suspicions, and induced him to inquire into her case, was certain prognostications made in Flanders of a conspiracy against the King's life by people, it was said, nearest to his Royal person. After which avowal, Cromwell went on to extol beyond measure the sense, the wit, and the courage of the deceased Royal mistress, as well as of her brother (George); (fn. n2) and, in order the more to persuade me, and instil hope of the good issue of our enterprise, he declared to me confidentially, and with the greatest possible reserve, that the King, his master, being perfectly aware of the wishes and affection of all his subjects, had decided at this next Parliament to have the Princess, his daughter, declared heiress to his crown.

Yet I must say, that, notwithstanding this asseveration of

Cromwell, the conversation I have since had with him, and of which more will be said hereafter, leaves one in doubt more than ever as to the veracity of his report; for he earnestly requested me, at my next audience from the King, not in anywise to allude to the Princess, and, if I did at all, not to designate her by that title. He told me further; he said that it was necessary before all things that the Princess should write a letter to her father according to a minute drawn up by him [Cromwell], which he then and there exhibited, and which, I must own, could not have been conceived in more honest or reasonable terms than it was. The better to persuade the Princess to do that which was required of her, he [Cromwell] had, at the King's express commands, sent to her a lady in her utmost confidence. At any rate, to do away with all scruples, if any remained on her part, the King proposed asking me to write to the Princess, and send the letter by one of my secretaries, begging her not to offer any difficulties, and subscribe at once to her father's wish in that respect. The Princess' letter would then be translated into English and Latin in order that I might see there was nothing in its contents that was not honest, just, and reasonable.

LETTER FROM CASTILLON (1538)

Louis de Perreau (c.1489–c.1547), Sieur de Castillon, was the French ambassador to England. He wrote this letter – revealing Henry VIII's capricious view of Cromwell even before his secretary fell from favour – to his friend Constable de Montmorency on 14 May 1538. (Castillon was succeeded as ambassador by de Marillac – see Chapter 13.)

After being three or four times at the Council, I found the lord Privy Seal [i.e. Cromwell] so opposed to my negotiation and so proud and ungracious, that I could not help telling the King one day that I did not seem to be before his Council but that of the Emperor, for I saw more debated for the Emperor than for him. He then reprimanded my lord Privy Seal, saying he was a good manager, but not fit to inter-meddle in the affairs of kings, and did no less to three or four others of the Council. He then sent for Norfolk, whom the lord Privy Seal prevented, as much as possible, from coming to Court. The said Lord is so snubbed and so suspect for the affairs of France, that for the present his advice is not much asked; and now most of the Court visit me, which is a good sign.

CROMWELL'S INJUNCTIONS (1538)

In 1538 Cromwell issued his second series of Royal Injunctions for church practice – these led to the creation of the parish register system which is still used today, although superseded by civil registration from 1837.

In the name of God, Amen. By the authority and commission of the excellent prince Henry, by the grace of God King of England and of France, defender of the faith, lord of Ireland, and in earth Supreme Head under Christ of the Church of England, I, Thomas lord Crumwel, lord privy seal, Vicegerent to the King's said highness for all his jurisdictions ecclesiastical within his realm, do for the true honour of Almighty God, increase of virtue, and discharge of the King's majesty, give and exhibit unto you—these injunctions following, to be kept, observed, and fulfilled, upon the pains hereafter declared.

    1. First, Ye shall truly observe and keep all and singular the King's Highness' Injunctions, given unto you heretofore in my name, by his Grace's authority; not only upon the pains therein expressed, but also in your default now after this second monition continued, upon further punishment to

be straitly extended towards you by the King's Highness' arbitrement, or his Vice-gerent aforesaid.

2. Item, That ye shall provide on this side the feast of Easter next coming, one book of the whole Bible of the largest volumeɪ in English, and the same set up in some convenient place within the said church that you have cure of, whereas your parishioners may most commodiously resort to the same and read it, the charge of which book shall be ratably born between you the parson and the parishioners aforesaid, that is to say one half by you, and the other half by them.

3. Item, That ye shall discourage no man privily or apertly from the reading or hearing of the said Bible, but shall expressly provoke, stir, and exhort every person to read the same, as that which is the very lively word of God, that every Christian man is bound to embrace, believe and follow if he look to be saved; admonishing them nevertheless to avoid all contention, altercation therein, and to use an honest sobriety in the inquisition of the true sense of the same, and refer the explanation of obscure places to men of higher judgement in Scripture.

4. Item, That ye shall every Sunday and holy-day through the year, openly and plainly recite to your parishioners, twice or thrice together, or oftener, if need require, one particle or sentence of the Pater Noster, or Creed, in English, to the intent that they may learn the same by heart; and so from day to day to give them one like lesson or sentence of the same, till they have learned the whole Pater Noster and Creed in English, by rote. And as they may be taught every sentence of the same by rote, ye shall expound and declare the understanding of the same unto them, exhorting all parents and householders to teach their children and servants the same, as they are bound in conscience to do. And that done, ye shall declare unto them the Ten Commandments, one by one,

every Sunday and holy-day, till they be likewise perfect in the same.

5. Item, That ye shall in confessions every Lent examine every person that comes to confession unto you, whether they can recite the Articles of our Faith, and the Pater Noster in English, and hear them say the same particularly; wherein if they be not perfect, ye shall declare to the same that every Christian person ought to know the same before they should receive the Blessed Sacrament of the Altar; and monish them ibid. to learn the same more perfectly by the next year following, or else, like as they ought not to presume to come to God's board without perfect knowledge of the same, and if they do, it is to the great peril of their souls; so ye shall declare unto them that ye look for other injunctions from the King's highness by that time, to stay and repel all such from God's board, as shall be found ignorant in the premises, whereof ye do thus admonish them, to the intent they should both eschew the peril of their souls, and also the worldly rebuke that they might incur hereafter by the same.

6. Item, That ye shall make, or cause to be made, in the said church, and every other cure ye have, one sermon every quarter of a year at the least, wherein ye shall purely and sincerely declare the very Gospel of Christ, and in the same exhort your hearers to the works of charity, mercy, and faith, specially prescribed and commanded in Scripture, and not to repose their trust and affiance in any other works devised by men's phantasies besides Scripture; as in wandering to pilgrimages, offering of money, candles, or tapers to images or relics, or kissing or licking the same, saying over a number of beads, not understood or minded on, or in such-like superstition; for the doing whereof, ye not only have no promise of reward in Scripture, but contrariwise, great threats and

maledictions of God, as things tending to idolatry and superstition, which of all other offences God Almighty doth most detest and abhor, for that the same diminished most His honour and glory.

7. Item, That such feigned images as ye know of in any of your cures to be so abused with pilgrimages or offerings of anything made thereunto, ye shall, for avoiding that most detestable sin of idolatry, forthwith takedown and delay, and shall suffer from henceforth no candles, tapers, or images of wax to be set afore any image or picture but only the light that commonly goeth across the church by the rood-loft, the light before the sacrament of the altar, and the light about the sepulchre, which for the adorning of the church and divine service ye shall suffer to remain; still admonishing your parishioners, that images serve for none other purpose but as to be books of unlearned men, that can no letters, whereby they might be otherwise admonished of the lives and conversation of them that the said images do represent; which images, if they abuse for any other intent than for such remembrances, they commit idolatry in the same, to the great danger of their souls : and therefore the King's Highness, graciously tendering the weal of his subjects' souls, hath in part already, and more will hereafter, travail for the abolishing of such images as might be an occasion of so great an offence to God, and so great a danger to the souls of his loving subjects.

8. Item, That in all such benefices or cures as ye have whereupon ye be not yourselves resident, ye shall appoint such curates in your stead, as both can by their ability, and will also promptly execute these injunctions, and do their duty; otherwise that ye are bound in every behalf accordingly, and may profit their cure, no less with good example of living, than with declaration of the word of God, or else their lack and defaults shall be imputed unto

you, who shall straitly answer for the same it they do otherwise.

9. That ye shall admit no man to preach within any your benefices or cures, but such as shall appear unto you to be sufficiently licensed thereunto by the King's Highness, or his Grace's authority, by the Archbishop of Canterbury, or the bishop of this diocese; and such as shall be so licensed, ye shall gladly receive to declare the word of God, without any resistance or contradiction.

10. Item, If ye have heretofore declared to your parishioners anything to the extolling or setting forth of pilgrimages, feigned relics, or images, or any such superstition, ye shall now openly afore the same recant and reprove the same, shewing them (as the truth is) that ye did the same upon no ground of Scripture, but as one being led and seduced by a common error and abuse crept into the church, through the sufferance and avarice of such as felt profit by the same.

11. Item, If ye do or shall know any man within your parish, or elsewhere, that is a letter of the word of God to be read in English or sincerely preached, or of the execution of these Injunctions, or a favourer of the Bishop of Rome's pretended power, now by the laws of this realm justly rejected and extirpated, ye shall detect and present the same to the King's Highness, or his honourable Council or to his vice-gerent aforesaid, or the justice of peace next adjoining.

12. Item, That you, and every parson, vicar, or curate within this diocese, shall for every church keep one book or register, wherein ye shall write the day and year of every wedding, christening, and burying, made within your parish for your time and so every man succeeding you likewise ; and also there insert every person's name that shall be so wedded, christened, or buried; and for the safe keeping of the same book, the parish shall be bound to

provide, of their common charges, one sure coffer with
two locks and keys whereof the one to remain with you,
and the other with the wardens of every such parish
wherein the book shall be laid up ; which book ye shall
every Sunday take forth, and in the presence of the said
wardens, or one of them, write and record in the same all
the weddings, christenings, and buryings, made the whole
week before; and that done to lay up the book in the said
coffer as before; and for every time that the same shall be
omitted, the party that shall be in the fault thereof shall
forfeit to the said church 3s-4d, to be employed on the
reparation of the same church.

13. Item, That ye shall once every quarter of a year read these
    and the other former Injunctions given unto you by the
    authority of the King's Highness, openly and deliberately
    before all your parishioners, to the intent that both you
    may be the better admonished of your duty, and your said
    parishioners the more incited to ensue the same for their
    part.

14. Item, Forasmuch as by a law established every man is
    bound to pay his tithes; no man shall by colour of duty
    omitted by their curates, retain their tithes and so redub
    one wrong with another, or be his own judge, but shall
    truly pay the same, as hath been accustomed, to their
    parsons and curates, without any restraint or diminution;'
    and such lack and default as they can justly find in their
    parsons and curates, to call for reformation thereof at their
    ordinaries' and other superiors' hands, who upon
    complaints and due proof thereof shall reform the same
    accordingly.

15. Item, That no person shall from henceforth alter or
    change the order and manner of any fasting-day that is
    commanded and indicted by the Church, nor of any
    prayer, or Divine Service, otherwise than is specified in the
    said Injunctions, until such time as the same shall be so

ordered and transposed by the King's Highness' authority; the eves of such saints, whose holy days be abrogated, only excepted, which shall be declared henceforth to be no fasting days; excepted, also the Commemoration of Thomas Becket, sometime Archbishop of Canterbury which shall be clean omitted, and instead thereof the ferial service used.

16. Item, That the knelling of the Aves after service, and certain other times, which hath been brought in and begun by the pretence of the Bishop of Rome's pardon, henceforth be left and omitted, lest the people do hereafter trust to have pardon for the saying of their Aves, between the said knelling, as they have done in time past.

17. Item, Where in times past men have used in divers places in their processions to sing Ora pro nobis to so many saints, that they had no time to sing the good suffrages following, as Parce nobis Domine and Libera nos Domine, it must be taught and preached that better it were to omit Ora pro nobis, and to sing the other suffrages.

18. All Which and singular Injunctions I minister unto you and your successors, by the King's Highness' authority to me committed in this part, which I charge and command you by the same authority to observe and keep, upon pain of deprivation, sequestration of the fruits or such other coercion as [to] the King's Highness, or his Vice-gerent for the time being, shall be seen convenient.

11

POLE'S APOLOGIA (1539)

Reginald Pole (1500–1558) was the last Catholic Archbishop of
Canterbury (from 1556 to 1558, under Mary I), and wrote extensive
works and correspondence about the religious turmoils of his era. He
was a great-nephew of Edward IV and Richard III. Pole notably disap-
proved of Henry VIII's marriage to Anne Boleyn. He was made a
cardinal in 1536, and then papal legate to England – he was a key
figure in the Counter-Reformation after Henry VIII's death. Pole's
Apologia ad Carolum Quintum, addressed to the Holy Roman Emperor
Charles V, was written in 1539 and expresses his theory that Machiavelli's *The Prince* was a key influence on Henry VIII breaking from
Rome, and that Cromwell was the conduit for this work.

*In this first passage from the Apologia, in a new translation from the orig-
inal Latin, Pole discusses Cromwell's background and his fate, and makes
his low opinion of Cromwell's machinations clear.*

So, then, if you ask for his name, they call it Cromwell; if you ask
which family it comes from, I hold that there was nobody famous
before him who bore this name. However, they say there is a small

village near London where he was born and where his father used to earn his crust by collecting cloth, but this is of no interest.

Now if the question is asked, as I have understood him, he was a soldier on foot in Italy; he was also a merchant, and yet he did not have success in trading longer than he had as a merchant scribe and as an auditor of books of accounts; I knew very well indeed that merchant, who was of Venetian nationality, with whom he placed his work.

Finally bored by this condition, and returned home, he mixed with lawyers, those who practised the law of the Kingdom. And in this area he hoped to have more results, since he was aware of his versatile and skilful ingenuity in defending both the unjust and the fair, since he had intensively perfected himself with the trade of other people's affairs, although he always paid little attention to the naivety of our wits. And yet he never distinguished himself particularly in this way, until he came to the Ruin of the Monasteries. And this began when the Cardinal of York [i.e. Thomas Wolsey] was still alive, until certain monasteries remained almost empty of their monks, and the possessions of those and their farms were given in support of the poor who had dedicated themselves to the study of letters in college. At this point he began to be known, and therefore was proven to be born only for this particular art: for the dismantling of the monasteries and for their devastation.

This was because a mutation of his other talents manifested itself, in which nothing progressed but in this instead he began to be famous immediately, and known to most, known in these beginnings of his art – so that, since the Cardinal, of whom he was a servant and from whose authority and from whose power he gained notoriety for that art of his, had been freed from State administration, and deprived of office, he [Cromwell] was sentenced to execution; this is according to the voice of all those who had known something about him.

In fact, I can say that I was present in London at the time, and I listened to the rumours, even to the point that a rumour was circulating throughout the city, according to which he had been thrown into prison, and soon he would have been led to execution. And in truth the people did not expect any more pleasant spectacle, and that rumour had not arisen from any other motivation, than because everyone knew that he deserved to be executed.

The translations from the Apologia *below are taken from Thomas Phillips'* *1765 translations in his* The History of the Life of Reginald Pole, *and* *explicitly refer to Cromwell being influenced by Machiavelli's The Prince, of* *which Pole had said: 'I found this type of book to be written by an enemy of* *the human race. It explains every means whereby religion, justice and any* *inclination toward virtue could be destroyed.'*

Some time after my return from Italy, I met [Cromwell] in the Cardinal of York's palace, in whose service he then was, and, after the usual compliments, he fell into a discourse on the necessary qualifications of those who are called to the Councils of Princes. His motive, I suppose, was to sift me concerning the Divorce, which then divided the Privy Council, as he knew my opinion of the affair could not fail of being asked. My answer was, that I thought it the duty of every such person, above all other considerations, to advise what was most conducing to his Prince's honour and interest, and enlarged myself, from the dictates of reason, and the best Authors, on the nature of Virtue, in which both honour and interest are grounded. He replied, that these notions were very plausible, when delivered in the schools or from the Pulpit, but were of little use in the Cabinets of Kings; and, if much insisted on, instead of being favourably heard, would create hatred and aversion to the Adviser, as they seldom fall in with the Prince's inclinations, and are quite foreign to what is practised in Courts. That Prudence and Experience chiefly discovered themselves in proposing what was seasonable as to time, place, and other circumstances: that men of letters were often deceived, and sell into disgrace for want of this knowledge: that those very things which a Prince would hear with approbation from a Preacher, would be rejected by him with disdain, is urged as the rule of his proceedings: that this was a Science which the Universities did not teach, and, therefore, those who came raw from them to the Council-board, were liable to great oversights. He strengthened what he was saying by the example of several, who, because they would not depart from the principles they had imbibed there, had forfeited their Prince's favour, were become useless, or had brought ruin on themselves and families. From whence he concluded, that the chief concern of a person in this station, should be to study his Prince's inclinations, in which much sagacity was required, as they sometimes lie disguised under appearances of a very different import: that it became Kings to use the specious names of religion, equity, and other virtues, though their designs were not always regulated by them: that true ability lay in discovering what these real intentions were; and, then, in managing affairs in such sort as they might obtain their ends, and yet no open failure in religion or probity be observed: and that this ability was seen in proportion as the Minister could reconcile the appearances of virtue, which Princes were unwilling to give up, with the substantial interest of the State. That this was a compendious way to secure savour and authority with them, and to be useful to one's self and others.

This was the sum of Cromwell's discourse, which was long; from whence I gathered, that, if he really thought as he spoke, and had been Nero's Counsellor, when the murder of his Mother was in debate; he, who acknowledged no law, when his Prince's inclination was to be gratified, and made religion and integrity bend to it, would not have been at a loss to justify that parricide.

However, I made no reply to this barefaced impiety, and only said, I imagined he had entered on the discourse for argument sake, and did not mean to deliver his real sentiments. He made no apology for any thing he had advanced; but perceiving, as well he might, both from my countenance and some words which dropped from me, that I was rather displeased than taken with his Politics, he replied, it was no wonder, if having, as yet, little use of public affairs, I did not comprehend what experience alone could teach; especially as it did not agree with those tenets, in which I had been brought up: but now, as I had done with books and retirement, if I would mix in public life and give myself to

business, I should see how wide a difference there was between the maxims of real policy, and those idle speculations, in which men, who have nothing else to do, descant in the Schools: that these were very unskilful Teachers of an Art, which could be learnt from Practice only; and that a short discourse of an experienced person was more to the purpose than whole Volumes of such Philosophers: that if I needs must have books, I should, at least, read those who allow more to experience than to speculation: that he had one os a very acute Modern, who did not, like Plato, publish his own dreams, and draw up the plan of a Commonwealth, which, for so many ages, had never been reduced to practice, but had laid down maxims and observations, of which daily experience confirmed the truth: and, if I would give him leave, and promise to read the book, he would send it me: that he had a great regard for me, and foresaw to what difficulties I should be exposed, if I let myself be carried away by motions of men unacquainted with the world, though otherwise, ever so learned; and had not a greater deference to those who had joined eminent parts to a habit of business. Having thanked him for his civilities, and promised to read the Work, we parted.

Soon after, the King not finding that compliance with his desires, even in those who were thought to have given occasion to them, which he expected, began to make use of this man's ill-fated abilities, and admit him to his most secret deliberations; and, then, the conversation, which had past between us, was a seasonable warning to me to fly an unhospitable shore. If any thing could give me a greater insight into his Character, it was the book itself, he so much extolled, though never sent me, I imagine he already repented having laid himself so open; but being informed of his private readings by those who were acquainted with them, I procured the Work, and was as eager to peruse it, as any one could be to intercept dispatches which discovered the designs of an Enemy. On reading it, I found, in effect, every stratagem by which religion, justice, and good faith were to be defeated, and every human and divine virtue become a prey to self-ishness, dissimulation, and falsehood. It was wrote by one Machiavel, a native of Florence, and intitled, On the Art of Government; and is such a performance, that was Satan himself to leave a Successor, I do not well see by what other maxims he would direct him to reign.

12

LETTER FROM CROMWELL (JULY 1540)

(Sent to Henry VIII from the Tower of London on 24 July 1540, four days before Cromwell's execution. Paragraph breaks have been added to aid reading, and the text transcribed into more modern English.)

Most gracious King and most merciful sovereign, your most humble, most obedient and most bounden subject and most lamentable servant and prisoner. Prostrate at the feet of your most excellent Majesty, I have heard your pleasure by the mouth of your Controller, which was that I should write to your most excellent Highness such things as I thought meet to be written concerning my most miserable state and condition for the which your most abundant goodness, benignity and licence the immortal God Three and One reward your majesty.

And now most gracious Prince, to the matter first whereas I have been accused to your Majesty of Treason – to that I say I never in all my life thought willingly to do anything that might or should displease your Majesty; and much less to do or say that thing which of itself is so high and abominable and offence as God knoweth (and who I doubt not shall reveal the truth to your Highness). Your Grace knows my accusers, God forgive them. For I ever always had love for your honour, person, life, prosperity, health, wealth, joy and comfort and also your most dear and entirely beloved Son the Prince, his Grace and your proceeding, God so help me in this my adversity, and confound me if ever I thought the contrary. What labours, pains and travails I have taken according to my most bounden duty, God also knoweth, for if it were in my power to make your Majesty to live ever young and prosperous, God knows I would; or if it had been or were in my power to make your Majesty so puissant that all the world should be compelled to obey you, Christ knows I would, for so I am of all others most bounden.

For your Majesty hath been the most bountiful prince to me that ever was king to his subject, yea, and more like a dear father than a master. Such hath been your most grace and goodly counsels towards me at sundry times, that I ask your mercy where I have offended. Shall I now despite such exceeding goodness and bounty be your traitor, nay, then the greatest pains were too little for me. Should any faction or any affection make me a traitor to your Majesty, then all the devils in Hell confound me and the vengeance of God light upon me if I should once have thought it, most gracious Sovereign.

I never spoke with the Chancellor of the Augmentations and Frogmerton [i.e. Sir George Throgmorton] together at one time; but if I did, I never spoke of any such matter. Your Grace knows what manner of man Throgmerton has ever been towards you and your proceedings. What Master Chancellor has been to me, God and he know best, I will not accuse him. What I have been to him, your Majesty well knows. I would to Christ I had obeyed your Grace's frequent counsels and warnings then it would not have been with me as now it is. Yet our Lord, if it be his will, can do with me as he did with Susan who was falsely accused. I have committed my soul, my body and goods to God, at your Majesty's pleasure, in whose mercy and pity I do wholly repose. For other hope than in God and your Majesty I have not.

Sir, as to your Commonwealth, I have after my wit, power and knowledge travailed therein, doing my duty to the same having no respect to persons (your Majesty only excepted), and I trust God shall bear me witness that the world cannot justly accuse me of having done any injustice or wrong wilfully. And yet I have not done my duty in all things as I was bound, wherefore I ask mercy. If I have heard of any combinations, conventicles or offenders against your laws, I have for the most part revealed them and also caused them to be punished, not of malice, as God shall judge me. Nevertheless, Sire, I have meddled in so many matters under your Highness that I am not able to answer them all – but one thing I am well assured of is that that I have never wittingly or willingly thought to offend your Highness. Still, hard it is for me or any other meddling as I have done to live under your Grace and your laws, but we must daily offend, and where I have offended, I most humbly ask mercy and pardon at your gracious will and pleasure.

Amongst other things, most gracious sovereign, Master Controller showed me that you complained that within these 14 days I revealed a matter of great secrecy contrary to your expectation. Sire, I do well remember the matter, but I never revealed it to any creature except after your Grace had opened the matter first to me in your chamber decrying your lamentable fate. You declared the thing which your Highness misliked in the Queen, at which time I told your Grace that she often desired to speak with me but I durst not. You said why should I not, alleging that I might do much good in going to her and to be plain with her in declaring my mind. Lacking opportunity, I spoke with her lord Chamberlain, for which I ask your Grace's mercy, desiring him – not naming your Grace to him – to find some means that the Queen might be induced to behave pleasantly towards you. I thought thereby to have some faults amended to your Majesty's comfort. I repeated the suggestion, when the said lord Chamberlain and others of the Queen's council came to me in my chamber at Westminster for licence for the departure of the strange maidens. I then required them to counsel their mistress to use all pleasantness to your Highness. This was before your Grace committed the secret matter to me, and only so that she might have been induced to such pleasant and honourable fashions as might have been to your Grace's comfort which above all things, as God knoweth, I did most court and desire.

After that time, I never disclosed to any but my lord Admiral, which I did by your Grace's commandment on Sunday last; whom I found equally willing to seek a remedy for your comfort and consolation. I saw by him that he did as much lament your Highness' fate as ever did man, and was wonderfully grieved to see your Highness so troubled, wishing greatly your comfort and saying he would spend the best blood in his belly for that object. And if I would not do the same and willingly die for your comfort, I would I were in Hell and I receive a thousand deaths. Sire, this is all that I have done in this matter and if I have offended your Majesty therein, prostrate at your feet I most lowly ask mercy and pardon of your Highness.

Sire, there was also laid unto my charge at my examination that I had retained contrary to your laws. Sire, what exposition may be made upon retainers I know not, but this I will say: if I ever retained any man other than those as were in my household servants, it was against my will. But most gracious Sovereign, I have been so called on and besought by them that said they were my friends that, constrained thereunto, I received their children and friends – not as retainers, for their fathers and parents did promise to me to find them and so I took them not as retainers to my great charge and for non- evil as God best knows. I most humbly beseech your Majesty of pardon if I have offended therein. Sire, I do acknowledge myself to have been a most miserable and wretched sinner and that I have not toward God and your Highness behaved myself as I ought and should have done. For the which, my offence to God while I live I shall continually call for his mercy, and for my offences to your Grace – which God knows were neither malicious nor wilfull, and that I never thought treason to your Highness, your realm, or posterity, so God help me, either in word or deed. Nevertheless, prostrate at your Majesty's feet, in whatsoever thing I have offended, I appeal to your Highness for mercy, grace and pardon in such ways as shall be your pleasure.

Beseeching the almighty maker and redeemer of this world to

send your Majesty continual and long health, wealth and prosperity with Nestor's years to reign, and your most dear son the Prince's Grace to prosper, reign and continue long after you – and to anyone who would wish the contrary, a short life, shame and confusion.

Written with the quaking hand and most sorrowful heart of your most sorrowful subject, and most humble servant and prisoner, this Saturday at your Tower of London.

– Thomas Crumwell

13

LETTERS FROM DE MARILLAC (1540–1)

Charles de Marillac (c.1510–1560) was a French priest and diplomat, sent to England in 1538, where he remained for five years. His dispatches to France detail Henry's meeting with and disdain for Anne of Cleves, and the downfall of Thomas Cromwell.

10 April 1540

To Anne de Montmorency [supervisor of the royal household of the French king, Francis I]

The farce of which I have already written has been still better played by those who, after encouraging the doctors at whose preaching they despoiled the abbeys, and took the wealth of the Church, now procure the ruin of the said doctors, who lay the blame upon them — amongst others upon Cromwell and the archbishop of Canterbury, who do not know where they are. Within few days there will be seen in this country a great change in many things; which this King begins to make in his ministers, recalling those he had rejected and degrading those he had raised. Cromwell is tottering, for all those recalled, who were dismissed by his means, reserve 'une bonne pensee' [a good thought] for him; among others the bishops of Hoyncester, Durans and Belde [Barnes, Gerrard and Jerome], men of great learning and experience, who are now summoned to the Privy Council. It is said on good authority that Tonstallus, bishop of Durans, a person in great esteem with the learned, shall be vicar general of the spiritualty, and that the bishop of Belde [Bath] shall be keeper of the Privy Seal, which are Cromwell's two principal titles. In any case, the name of vicar general will not remain to him, as even his own people assert. If he remains in his former credit and authority it will only be because he is very assiduous in affairs, although rough in his management of them, and that he does nothing without first consulting the King, and also shows himself willing to do justice, especially to foreigners.

c.17 April 1540

Cromwell's biographer Roger Merriman cites de Marillac reporting a week later than the above letter that Cromwell:

... was in as much credit with the King as ever he was, from which he was near being shaken by the Bishop of Winchester and others.

[No source given.]

23 June 1540

Marillac to Francis I

Yesterday, presented to this King his letters of credence touching Cromwell, and spoke of the harm done by such a minister, and the expediency of taking him away before he had completed his unhappy designs. He took it in good part...

Same date, Marillac to Montmorency

Had their posts made as good speed as the English courier, Montmorency should have known of the taking of Cromwell as soon as Wallop did. Nothing else is spoken of here, and in a week at latest the said prisoner is expected to be executed and treated as be deserves, as appears by the presages and arguments here following.

To commence with the day of his taking in the Council Chamber of the King's house at Westminster:— As soon as the Captain of the Guard declared his charge to make him prisoner, Cromwell in a rage cast his bonnet on the ground, saying to the duke of Norfolk and others of the Privy Council assembled there that this was the reward of his services, and that he appealed to their consciences as to whether he was a traitor; but since he was treated thus he renounced all pardon, as he had never thought to have offended, and only asked the King not to make him languish long. Thereupon some said he was a traitor, others that he should be judged according to the laws he had made, which were so sanguinary that often words spoken inadvertently with good intention had been constituted high treason. The duke of Norfolk having reproached him with some villainies done by him, snatched off the order of St. George which he bore on his neck, and the Admiral, to show himself as great an enemy in adversity as he had been thought a friend in prosperity, untied the Garter. Then, by a door which opens upon the water, he was put in a boat and taken to the Tower without the people of this town suspecting it until they saw all the King's archers under Mr. Cheyney at the door of the prisoner's house, where they made an inventory of his goods, which were not of such value as people thought, although too much for a *compaignon de telle estoffe*. The money was £7,000... and the silver plate, including crosses, chalices, and other spoils of the Church might be as much more. These movables were before night taken to the King's treasury — a sign that they will not be restored.

Next day were found several letters he wrote to or received from the Lutheran lords of Germany. Cannot learn what they contained except that this King was thereby so exasperated against him that he would no longer hear him spoken of, but rather desired to abolish all memory of him as the greatest wretch ever born in England. To commence, this King distributed all his offices and proclaimed that none should call him lord Privy Seal or by any other title of estate, but only Thomas Cromwell, shearman [*tondeur de draps* – cutter of cloth, alluding to Cromwell's humble background], depriving him of all his privileges and prerogatives, and distributing his less valuable moveables among his [Cromwell's] servants, who were enjoined no longer to wear their master's livery. From this it is inferred that he will not be judged with the solemnity accustomed to be used to the lords of this country, nor beheaded; but will be dragged up as an ignoble person, and afterwards hanged and quartered. A few days will show; especially as they have determined to empty the Tower at this Parliament, which finishes with this month...

It remains to name those who have succeeded to Cromwell's estates. Will not depict those whom Montmorency knows already. The Admiral is made lord Privy Seal, and lord Russell Admiral; the bishop of Durham is first secretary; of the office of vicar as to the spiritualty, no decision has yet been come to, but people say that if one is made it will be the bishop of Winchester, who, since the imprisonment of his great adversary, has been called to the Privy Council, which, before, he was not accustomed to enter. For affairs of justice they have deputed the Chancellor, who, among other virtues, can neither speak French nor Latin, and has the reputation of being a good seller of justice whenever he can find a buyer...

3 March 1541

Marillac to Montmorency

Received, two days ago, a packet from the Court, in which were only two little letters from the Chancellor, written at Chambourg [Chambord], 21 and 22 Feb....

With regard to his letter to the King, this King's life was really thought to be in danger, not from the fever but from the leg, which often troubles him because he is very stout and marvellously excessive in drinking and eating, so that people worth credit say he is often of a different opinion in the morning than after dinner. Directs attention to the instability of the people and this King's impression of his ministers, whom (besides what Marillac writes to the King) he sometimes even reproaches with Cromwell's death, saying that, upon light pretexts, by false accusations, they made him put to death the most faithful servant he ever had.

14

LETTER FROM HILLES (1541)

Richard Hilles (c.1514–1587) was a merchant, and a co-founder of the Merchant Taylors' School. A Protestant, he had sought support from Cromwell. He later went into exile from 1539 to 1548. The extract below is from a letter to the Swiss church reformer Heinrich Bullinger (1504–1575), dated 28 February 1541.

At the beginning of June Cromwell was sent to the Tower, from whence he never went forth till 28 July, when he was beheaded with lord Hungerford, who was charged with attempting to compute the day of the King's death. I know nothing for certain of the cause of Cromwell's execution, but probably it was for not supporting the divorce as Winchester and others did. Not long before his death the King had granted him great additional houses and lands and offices, just as he endowed queen Anne before he beheaded her. But some think this was an artifice to make people think he had been guilty of the most heinous treason; and some think it was a like artifice in the King to confer his title and many of his domains while he was yet in prison upon his son Gregory, who was almost a fool, in order that he might the more readily confess his offences at execution. Others, however, say that he was threatened with burning at the stake instead of death by the axe if he did not confess his crimes at execution, and that he then said he was a miserable sinner against God and the King, but that what he said of having offended the King he said carelessly and coldly.

Our sins have doubtless deserved this change. Those on whose support we depended for purity of doctrine have been removed; for we have placed too much confidence in individuals, and now God has taken them all away, so that a man may travel from the East of England to the West and from the North to the South, without being able to discover a single preacher who, out of a pure heart and with faith unfeigned, is seeking the glory of God. He has taken them all away – Queen Anne, who was beheaded, with her brother, Cromwell, Latimer, and the other bishops...

In the same Parliament, too, the King published a general pardon for all offences committed before 1 July 1540, except those against the royal person, wilful murders, &c. But it was provided that it should not extend to Cromwell, Barnes, Garrard, Jerome, nor to the two sons of the marquis of Exeter and of lord Montague.

HALL'S CHRONICLE (1548)

Edward Hall (c.1496–1547) was an English historian, member of parliament and lawyer, remembered for his *The Union of the Two Noble and Illustre Families of Lancastre and Yorke* — usually known as *Hall's Chronicle*. It was first published posthumously in 1548, and was a prime source for Shakespeare's history plays. (The years given below are based on the regnal years of Henry VIII, running from 22 April of the first year to 21 April of the second.)

1529–30

So he made great provision to go Northwarde and appareled his servauntes newly and bought many costely thinges for his houshould and so he might wel inough, for he had of the kynges gentlenes the bishopprickes of Yorke and Win- chester, which wer no smal thinges, but at this time divers of his servauntes departed from him to the kynges service, and in especiall Thomas Crumwel one of his chief counsayle and chefe doer for him in the suppression of abbeis. After that al thinges necessarie for his jornay wer prepared, he toke his jorney nortward til he came to South wel whiche is in his dioces and their he continued this yere ever grudgyng at his fall as you shall here after : but the landes whiche he had geven to his Colleges in Oxforde and Ypswych, were now come to the kinges handes, by his atteinder in the premunire, and yet the kyng of his gentlenes and for favour that he bare to good learnyng erected agayne the College in Oxford, and where it was named the Cardinalles College, he called it the kynges College, and endewed it with faire possessions, and put in newe statutes and ordinaunces, and for because the College of Ypswich was thought to be nothing profitable, therefore he lefte that dissolved.

1532–33

After the kyng perceiving his newe wife Quene Anne, to bee greate with childe, caused all officers necessary, to bee appoynted to her, and so on Easter even, she went to her Closet openly as Quene, with all solempnitie, and then the kyng appoynted the daie of her Coronacion, to bee kept on Whitsondaie next folowyng, and writynges were sent to all Shrives, to certifie the names of menne of fourtie pounde, to receive the Ordre of knighthod, or els to make a fyne : the assessement of whiche fines, were appoynted to Thomas Cromwell, Master of the Kynges Juell house, and counsailer to the Kyng, and newly in his hygh favour, whiche so pollityquely handeled the matter, that he raised of that sessyng of fines, a great somme of money to the kynges use : Also the kyng wrote letters to the citie of London, to prepare pagiauntes, against the same coronacion.

1535–6

In the beginnynge of this yere the Duke of Norffolke and the Byshop of Ely went to Caleys, and thether came the Admyral of Fraunce. And the xix. day of June was thre Monkes of the Charterhouse hanged, drawen, and quartred at Tyborne and their quarters set up about London for deniyng the kyng to be supreme head of the Churche. Their names were Exmewe, Myddlemore, and Nudigate. These men when they were arreigned at Westminster, be- haved them selfes very stifly and stubbornly, for hearyng their inditement red how trayterously they had spoken against the kynges Majestic his croune and dignitye, they neyther blushed nor bashed at it, but very folishly and hipocritically knowleged their treason whiche maliciously they avouched, havynge no lernyng for their defence, but rather beyng asked dyvers questions, they used a malicious silence, thinkyng as by their examinacions after warde in the Tower of London it dyd appeare, for so they sayed, that they thought those men whiche was the Lorde Crumwell and other that there satte upon them in judgement to be heretiques and not of the Churche of God, and therfore not worthy to be either aunswered or spoken unto. And therfore as they deserved, they received as you have heard before.

1537–8

Thys yere at the feaste of S. George, was the Lorde Cromewell made knyght of the Gartier.

1538–9

In thys moneth of Auguste, the Kynge of Scottes maryed the ladye Mary late Duches of Longvile. And in Septembre by the speciall mocyon of the Lorde Cromewell all the notable Images unto the whiche were made anye speciall Pilgrimages and Offerynges, were utterly taken away, as the Images of Walsyngham, Ypswyche, Worceter, the Ladye of Wilsdon, wyth manye other. And lykewyse the Shrines of counterfeated Sainctes, as the Shrine of Thomas Becket and dyverse other. And even forth wyth by the meanes of the saied Cromwell, al the ordres of supersticious and beggyng Freers, as White, Gray, Black, Augustine, Croched Freers, and likewise al the puling Nonnes, with their Cloisters and houses wer suppressed and put doune.

1539–40

And beside this, to have all his people in a redynesse, he directed his commissions thorough out the realme to have his people mustered, and the harneis and weapons sene and viewed, to thentent that all thynges should be in a redinesse if his enemies would make any attempt into this Realme : And amongest other, one commission was directed to the right worshipfull sir William Forman knight Maior of London and his brethren, for to certifie all the names of all men betwene the ages of Ix. and xvi. and the nomber of harnesses, weapons, with their kyndes and diversities : whereupon the said lord Maior and his brethren, every one havyng with them one of the counsaill or learned men of the citie repaired to their wardes, and there by the othe of the common counsaill and Constables of the same warde toke the nomber of the men, harnesses and weapons, according to their commission. And after that they had well viewed their Bookes and the nomber of the persones, they thought it not expedient to admit the whole nomber of suche as were certefied for able and apte persones for to Muster : Wherfore then they assembled theim selfes againe and chose out the moste able persones and put by thother, and specially al suche as had no harnesse, nor for whom no harnesse could be provided. But when they were credibly advertysed by the kynges Counsellour Thomas lord Cromewell knyght of the Noble Ordre of the Gartier Lorde Prevye Scale (to whose prudence and goodnesse the Citie was muche bounden) that the kyng hymselfe woulde see the people of the Citie Muster in a convenient nomber, and not to set furthe all their power, but to leave some at home to kepe the Citie. Then eftsones every Alderman repayred to hys warde, and there put asyde all suche as hadde Jackes, coates of plate, coates of mayle and bryganders, and appoynted none but suche as had whyte Harnesse, excepte suche as should beare Morysh Pyckes, whiche had no harnesse but skulles : and they appoynted none but suche as had white harnesse, neither dyd they admyt any that was a Straunger, although they were Denyzens. When it was knowen that the kyng would see the Muster, Lorde howe glad the people were to prepare, and what desyre they had to do their Prince service, it would have made any faithfull subjectes harte to have rejoysed. Then every man beyng of any substaunce provided hymself a coate of whyte silke, and garnyshed their bassenettes with turves lyke cappes of sylke, set with ouches, furnyshed with chaines of gold and fethers : other gylted their harnesse, their halberdes and pollaxes. Some, and especiall certayne goldsmythes had their brest plates yea and their whole harnesse of sylver bullion. The Constables were all in Jornettes of white silke with chaines and battel Axes. The meaner sort of people were all in coates of white cloth very curiously trimmed with the armes of the citie before and behinde. The lord Maier hymself was in a faire Armour, the crestes therof were gylt, and over that a coate of blacke velvet with half sieves, and so was sir Roger Cholmley knight Recorder of London and al thother Aldermen and Shiriffes and such as had bene shirifes, al wel mounted on stirring horses richely trapped covered, with battel axes in their handes and Mases and chaines about their neckes. The lorde Mayer had iiii. fotemen all in white silke, cutte, ruffed and pounced : he had also ii. Pages well mounted on stirring coursers, richely trapped and appareled in coates of Crimosyn velvet and cloth of golde paled, with chaynes of gold, the one bearyng his Helme and the other his Axe. He had also xvi. tall men on foote with gilte halbardes, whose doubletz were white silke, and hosen doublettes and shoes all whyte, cut after the Almayne fassion, puffed and pulled out with red sarcenet, every one havyng a whyte lether Jerkyn all to cutte and chaines about their neckes, with fethers and broches on their cappes. The Recorder and every Alderman had about hym iiii. Halbardes trymmed warlike.

1540–1

The xviii. daie of April, at Westminster was Thomas lorde Cromewell, created Erie of Essex, and made greate Chamber- lain of England, whiche ever the Erles of Oxenford had, whiche promocions he enjoyed short tyme, as after in the next yere maie appere...

The xix. day of July, Thomas lorde Cromewel, late made erle of

Essex, as before you have hard, beyng in the counsail chamber, was sodainly apprehended, and committed to the tower of London, the whiche many lamented, but mo rejoysed, and specially suche, as ether had been religious men, or favored religious persones, for thei banqueted, and triumphed together that night, many wisshyng that that daie had been seven yere before, and some fearyng least he should escape, although he were imprisoned, could not be mery. Other who knewe nothyng but truth by hym, bothe lamented hym, and hartely praied for hym : But this is true that of certain of the Clergie, he was detestably hated, and specially of suche as had borne swynge, and by his meanes was put from it, for in deede he was a man, that in all his doynges, semed not to favor any kynde of Popery, nor could not abide the snoffyng pride of some prelates, which undoubtedly whatsoever els was the cause of his death, did shorten his life, and procured the ende that he was brought unto : whiche was that the xix. daie of the saied monethe, he was attaynted by Parliament, and never came to his answere, whiche lawe many reported, he was the causer of the makyng thereof, but the truthe thereof I knowe not : The Articles for whiche he died, appereth in the Record, where his attaynder is written, whiche are to long to bee here rehersed, but to conclude he was there attainted of heresy, and high treason. And the xxviii. daie of July was brought to the skaffold on the tower hill, where he saied these wordes folowyng.

I am come hether to dye, and not to purge my self, as maye happen, some thynke that I will, for if I should so do, I wer a very wretche and miser : I am by the Lawe condempned to die, and thanke my lorde God that hath appoynted me this deathe, for myne offence : For sithence the tyme that I have had yeres of discretion, I have lived a synner, and offended my Lorde God, for the whiche I aske hym hartely forgevenes. And it is not unknowne to many of you, that I have been a greate traveler in this worlde, and beyng but of a base degree, was called to high estate, and sithens the tyme I came therunto, I have offended my prince, for the whiche I aske hym hartely forgevenes, and beseche you all to praie to God with me, that he will forgeve me. O father forgeve me. O sonne forgeve me, O holy ghost forgeve me : O thre persons in one God forgeve me. And now I praie you that be here, to beare me record, I die in the Catholike faithe, not doubtyng in any article of my faith, no nor doubtyng in any Sacrament of the Churche. Many hath sclaundered me, and reported that I have been a bearer, of suche as hath mainteigned evill opinions, whiche is untrue, but I confesse that like as God by his holy spirite, doth instruct us in the truthe, so the devill is redy to seduce us, and I have been seduced : but beare me witnes that I dye in the Catholicke faithe of the holy Churche. And I hartely desire you to praie for the Kynges grace, that he maie long live with you, in healthe and prosperitie. And after him that his sonne prince Edward, that goodly ympe, maie long reigne over you. And once again I desire you to pray for me, that so long as life remaigneth in this fleshe, I waver nothyng in my faithe.

And then made he his praier, whiche was long, but not so long, as bothe Godly and learned, and after committed his soule, into the handes of God, and so patiently suffered the stroke of the axe, by a ragged and Boocherly miser, whiche very ungoodly perfourmed the Office.

THE SPANISH CHRONICLE (BEFORE 1552)

The author of *The Chronicle of King Henry VIII. of England: Being a Contemporary Record of Some of the Principal Events of the Reigns of Henry VIII and Edward VI* (*Cronico del Rey Enrico Otavo de Inglaterra* in the original), known as the *Spanish Chronicle*, is unknown, and not regarded as historically very accurate (not least because it has the wrong order for Henry's wives) – although its account of Cromwell's last days is close to de Marillac's (see Chapter 13). The *Chronicle* was written before 1552 and translated into English in 1889 by the historian Martin Hume.

CHAPTER XII

HOW THE KING APPOINTED FOR HIS SECRETARY CROMWELL, WHO HAD BEEN SECRETARY OF THE ENGLISH CARDINAL.

When the King dismissed the Cardinal [Wolsey] from the Chancellorship, this Cardinal had a secretary called Cromwell, who at the time of the dismissal was going through all the abbeys in England, by orders of the Cardinal, to inquire the amounts of their income. This Cromwell was so diligent that he managed to inquire into everything, and the poor abbots, in doubt what was the object, and in the hope of ingratiating themselves with the Cardinal, sent him large sums of money by Cromwell, and when he arrived in London with the treasure, there was no lack of people to tell the King about it.

As soon as the King knew that this Cromwell had brought with him so much money robbed from the abbeys, the King sent for him, and said to him, 'Come hither; what are these robberies you have committed in the abbeys?' and Cromwell answered him very boldly, 'May it please your Majesty, I have not committed any robbery, and I have done nothing but what I was ordered to do by my master the Cardinal. The money I bring was sent of their own free will by the abbots of the monasteries as a gift to the Cardinal, and your Majesty well knows that the Cardinal did as he liked, and I did as he told me, and therefore I bring these thirty thousand pounds sterling for the Cardinal.'

The King thereupon took a great fancy to this Cromwell, and spoke to him in this fashion, 'Go to, Cromwell, thou art much cleverer than anyone thinks,' and instead of sending him to be hanged as everybody expected, he gave him a slap on the shoulder and said to him, 'Henceforward thou shalt be my secretary.' This was the beginning of the rise of this Cromwell, who afterwards became more powerful than the Cardinal himself, as we will tell further on.

Seeing himself so quickly raised to the place of secretary to the King, and being one of the greatest heretics in the kingdom, he determined to maintain his position and try to rise, so he said to the King, who he saw was bent upon aggrandizing the Crown, 'May it please your Majesty, I have a note of all the revenues and treasures held by the abbeys, and it seems to me that your Majesty could take away a great many of them, and apply the revenues to the crown.'

'But how can this be done, Cromwell?' said the King.

'I will tell your Majesty. I will present a letter to Parliament in your name asking them to grant you all the abbeys which have less than three thousand ducats, and your Majesty can then appropriate a great revenue to the Crown, and send the abbots to the richer abbeys.'

As this Cromwell had the revenues of the abbeys all written down, and signed by the abbots themselves, they could not get out of it. They were great simpletons, for a large proportion of them had signed that their abbeys did not reach three thousand ducats.

The petition was made to Parliament, and all declared in one voice that as the King was head of the Church he could do what he liked in his own Churchy and therefore the demand was granted.

Cromwell was no sluggard, for he immediately sent collectors to unmake the abbeys. A great quantity of plate and revenues was got from them, without counting the large quantity stolen by the Commissioners, and great was the damage done to the realm by the destitution of these abbeys.

After a time, to complete the work, they ordered that all the abbeys should be abolished; and as the King made grants to many gentlemen of the church buildings, which were all covered with lead, they consented the more readily, and did not see the great destruction that was coming to the country. For everyone who reads this must know that two-thirds of the nation were maintained by the abbeys, which had many estates, and let the land cheaply to farmers, who thus held their pastures on easy terms, whereas, when the estates came into the possession of the King, and the gentlemen began to buy the hereditaments of him, they let them very much dearer to the poor farmers, and thus commenced the great rise in the price of all victuals and other things, as will be told.

CHAPTER XV

HOW CROMWELL ADVISED THE KING TO ABOLISH THE MONASTERIES FROM THE KINGDOM.

This Cromwell was always inventing means whereby the King might be enriched and the crown aggrandized, and one day seeing the King in a good and merry humour, he said, 'I beseech your Majesty to listen to me,' to which the King answered, 'secretary, speak your will.'

'Then,' answered he, 'your Majesty should know that it will be well to abolish the monasteries. The many parish churches are quite enough, and so many distinctions of dress are not in accordance with the teaching of St. Peter.'

The King asked how it could be done, and Cromwell answered him: 'I will tell your Majesty; I will send to all the monasteries to order and give them notice that it is your wish that in future they should appear simply as priests, and then, after a little time, it can be done easily and without scandal, because as they will be dressed simply as clergymen, people will not see that they have been friars.'

The King answered, 'Do as you will, Cromwell; what you desire shall be carried out.'

Thereupon Cromwell sent to all the monasteries, and ordered them in the name of the King to go dressed as priests, and that all should change their monastic garb within one month. The sinners of friars, seeing this would give them more liberty, were in such a hurry to change that in a week there was not a friar to be seen, for they all appeared as priests, and in six months nobody knew that there had ever been any friars. When Cromwell saw that the time was ripe, he sent all over the kingdom and arranged that on a certain appointed day they should all be turned out of the monasteries, and thus was it done. Here the King got a great treasure in crosses, chalices, and vestments from the monasteries, and the poor priests who had been friars did not know what to do; so most of them went to the north, where they did what will be related further on.

CHAPTER XVII

HOW THE PRIESTS WHO HAD BEEN FRIARS WENT TO THE
NORTH, AND WHAT THEY DID.

When the poor friars saw themselves homeless, destitute, and
without food, most of them went to the north and stirred up the
common people to rise against the King. They chose for their leader a
lawyer named Aske, and met in a field, where one of the priests
preached a sermon, and in less than a week they were joined by forty
thousand men or more, and then chose their captains. This Aske was
their general... [This refers to the lawyer Robert Aske, 1500-1537, and
his contribution to the Pilgrimage of Grace, the rebellion in northern
England against the split from the Church of Rome, the Dissolution
of the Monasteries and Cromwell's policies.]

[The King]... sent Aske a prisoner to the city of York, and had him
hanged on the highest tower in the city so that all might see.

So ended Aske; and when it was all over, the King said to
Cromwell, 'It seems, Cromwell, that the country does not know thee
as I know thee. Whoever harms thee shall harm me.'

Then Cromwell knelt and kissed his hand. In short, this Cromwell
had more command even than the Cardinal had had, and the
gentlemen [i.e. the Council] obeyed him as if he were the King. If his
pride had not betrayed him, and he had kept friendly with the lords,
he would not have come to the end he did, as will be related
presently.

CHAPTER XXII

HOW PARLIAMENT MET, AND HOW THROUGH THE ADDRESS
DRAWN UP BY CROMWELL PRINCESS ELIZABETH WAS
ACKNOWLEDGED, AND MADAM MARY DECLARED A
BASTARD.

Within the time ordered by the King the Lords spiritual and temporal, together with all the Commons, met in the great hall at Westminster; and Cromwell was wide awake, and drew up an address to
present to Parliament, in which the following words were contained:
'Gentlemen, it is known to you how, by divine inspiration, his Majesty
the King has freed himself from the great sin in which he lived, and
how God has vouchsafed him fruit of grace. You also know how his
Majesty desires to do nothing without consulting you, and out of the
great love he bears his subjects he has called you here together to tell
you that Madam Mary is born of mortal sin, and as you swore allegiance to her without knowing of this obstacle, the King now wishes
you to declare her illegitimate, and that Madam Elizabeth be
acknowledged as princess.'

The Lords, as they all knew the King's will, waited for the
Commons to answer, and for a long while nobody spoke, but all held
their peace. As Cromwell saw that no one had anything to say, he
raised his voice so that all could hear, and spoke as follows: 'Then,
gentlemen, you will show the love you bear your King, and your will-
ingness to do as he wishes.' They all cried out in one voice, both
Lords and Commons, that the will of the King should be done, and
that they were ready to swear whenever they were ordered to do so.

CHAPTER XXVII

HOW CROMWELL TOOK MARK TO LONDON AND LEARNT
FROM HIM WHAT HAD HAPPENED.
(Mark Smeaton, c.1512-1536, was a court musician who was accused of
adultery with Anne Boleyn, as related in the chapter before this one.)

The night before they held the jousts the King came to Greenwich,
and all the gentlemen were very gay, particularly Master Norris and
Master Brereton. On the day of the jousts, which was the 1st of May,
Cromwell was going to London and sent for Mark, and said, 'Mark,
come and dine with me, and after dinner we will return together.'
Mark, suspecting nothing, accepted the invitation; and when they
arrived at Cromwell's house in London, before dinner, he took
Mark by the hand and led him into his chamber, where there were
six gentlemen of his, and as soon as he had got him in the chamber
he said, 'Mark, I have wanted to speak to you for some days, and I
have had no opportunity till now. Not only I, but many other
gentlemen, have noticed that you are ruffling it very bravely of late.
We know that four months ago you had nothing, for your father
has hardly bread to eat, and now you are buying horses and arms,
and have made showy devices and liveries such as no lord of rank
can excel. Suspicion has arisen either that you have stolen the
money or that someone had given it to you, although it is a great
deal for anyone to give unless it were the King or Queen, and the
King has been away for a fortnight. I give you notice now that you
will have to tell me the truth before you leave here, either by force
or goodwill.'

Mark, understanding as soon as Cromwell began to speak that the
affair was no joke, did not know what to say, and became confused.
'You had better tell the truth willingly,' said Cromwell; and then Mark
said that the money had been lent to him; to which Cromwell
answered, 'How can that be, that the merchants lend so much money,
unless on plate, gold, or revenue, and at heavy interest, whilst you

have nothing to pledge except that chain you wear. I am sorry you will not tell what you know with a good grace.'

Then he called two stout young fellows of his, and asked for a rope and a cudgel, and ordered them to put the rope, which was full of knots, round Mark's head, and twisted it with the cudgel until Mark cried out, 'sir Secretary, no more, I will tell the truth,' and then he said, 'The Queen gave me the money.'

'Ah, Mark,' said Cromwell, 'I know the Queen gave you a hundred nobles, but what you have bought has cost over a thousand, and that is a great gift even for a Queen to a servant of low degree such as you. If you do not tell me all the truth I swear by the life of the King I will torture you till you do.'

Mark replied, 'sir, I tell you truly that she gave it to me.' Then Cromwell ordered him a few more twists of the cord, and poor Mark, overcome by the torment, cried out, 'No more, Sir, I will tell you everything that has happened.' And then he confessed all, and told everything as we have related it, and how it came to pass.

When the Secretary heard it he was terror-stricken, and asked Mark if he knew of anyone else besides himself who had relations with the Queen. Mark, to escape further torture, told all he had seen of Master Norris and Brereton, and swore that he knew no more. Then Cromwell wrote a letter to the King, and sent Mark to the Tower.

CHAPTER XXVIII

HOW CROMWELL WROTE TO THE KING, AND HOW THE QUEEN AND HER GENTLEMEN-IN-WAITING WERE ARRESTED.

The Secretary at once wrote to the King, and sent Mark's confession to him by a nephew of his called Richard Cromwell, the letter being conceived as follows: 'Your Majesty will understand that, jealous of your honour, and seeing certain things passing in your palace, I determined to investigate and discover the truth. Your Majesty will recollect that Mark has hardly been in your service four months and only has £100 salary, and yet all the Court notices his splendour, and that he has spent a large sum for these jousts, all of which has aroused suspicions in the minds of certain gentlemen, and I have examined Mark, who has made the confession which I enclose to your Majesty in this letter.'

When the King read this confession his meal did not at all agree with him; but, like a valiant prince, he dissembled, and presently ordered his boat to be got ready, and went to Westminster. He ordered that the jousts should not be stopped, but when the festivities were over that Master Norris and Brereton, and Master Wyatt, should be secretly arrested and taken to the Tower. The Queen did not know I the King had gone, and went to the balconies where the jousts were to be held, and asked where he was, and was told that he was busy.

Presently came all the gentlemen who were to ride, and Master Norris and Brereton came, looking very smart, and their servants in gay liveries; but the Queen looked, and not seeing Mark, asked why he had not come out. She was told that he was not there, but had gone to London, and had not come back. So the jousts began, and Master Wyatt did better than anybody.

This Master Wyatt [the poet Thomas Wyatt] was a very gallant gentleman, and there was no prettier man at Court than he was. When the jousts were finished and they were disarming, the captain of the guard came and called Master Norris and Master Brereton, and said to them, 'The King calls for you.' So they went with him, and a boat being in waiting, they were carried off to the Tower without anyone hearing anything about it. Then Cromwell's nephew said to Master Wyatt, 'sir, the Secretary, my master, sends to beg you to favour him by going to speak with him, as he is rather unwell, and is in London.' So Wyatt went with him.

It seems that the King sent to Cromwell to tell him to have Wyatt fetched in order to examine him. When they arrived in London Cromwell took Master Wyatt apart, and said to him, 'Master Wyatt, you well know the great love I have always borne you, and I must tell you that it would cut me to the heart if you were guilty in the matter of which I wish to speak.' Then he told him all that had passed; and Master Wyatt was astounded, and replied with great spirit, 'sir Secretary, by the faith I owe to God and my King and lord, I have no reason to distrust, for I have not wronged him even in thought. The King well knows what I told him before he was married.'

Then Cromwell told him he would have to go to the Tower, but that he would promise to stand his friend, to which Wyatt answered, 'I will go willingly, for as I am stainless I have nothing to fear.' He went out with Richard Cromwell, and nobody suspected that he was a prisoner; and when be arrived at the Tower Richard said to the captain of the Tower, 'sir Captain, Secretary Cromwell sends to beg you to do all honour to Master Wyatt.' So the captain put him into a chamber over the door, where we will leave him, to say how the Queen and the Duke her brother were arrested.

CHAPTER XL

HOW THE ARCHBISHOP OF CANTERBURY PREACHED THAT THERE WAS NO PURGATORY, AND THE SEASON WHY HE PREACHED IT.

Secretary Cromwell was always trying to find new ways for the King to get money, and, to carry out the scheme he had thought of, he went to the Archbishop of Canterbury [Thomas Cranmer, 1489–1556, the first Anglican archbishop], and said to him, 'My lord, I much wish you would preach some day to the people in such a way that they will be willing for the King to have the endowments for masses for the dead, for you know the Church has two-thirds of the kingdom.'

The Archbishop said, 'I will go to London next Friday, and will preach in the cathedral in a manner that will very shortly bring about our purpose.' When Friday came he went to St. Paul's, it being Lent, and mounted the pulpit and preached his sermon, saying, 'Good people, great is the deception you have laboured under hitherto, and all caused by the Bishop of Rome, in order to get the money out of you, which he extracted every year for his bulls, making believe that those who bought them took a soul out of purgatory. I tell you it is all a snare, and I will make good that after the soul leaves the body it goes direct to paradise or to hell. This being so, what necessity is there for masses for the dead, or of priests to say them? The money extracted for such a purpose would be better bestowed upon the poor, and those who are learned may come to my house, and there in conference I will prove to them the truth of what I say.'

He said other great heresies, which I do not repeat, to avoid scandal; and when the sermon was ended nothing else was talked about in London, and as they are a very changeable people, they soon gave credit to this heresy; and in three days many learned men met in the Archbishop's house, where there were great disputes, and at last they all came to the conclusion that there was a place where souls were in repose. So they agreed to give the King, as head of the Church, all the endowments left by the dead for memorial masses.

But, although they agreed to do it, it was not possible to do it so quickly as they thought, and not indeed during the life of King Henry. Orders were given that all over the country they should preach that there was no purgatory, and Cromwell hastened it on so much, that in a short time all the kingdom agreed that the endowments should be given up; of which I shall speak again, and tell how Cromwell tried to marry the King out of England.

CHAPTER XLI

HOW CROMWELL STROVE TO MARRY THE KING WITH ANNE OF CLEVES.

After the execution of Queen Katharine Howard [note: this is incorrect, as Henry married Katherine Howard after Anne of Cleves!] Secretary Cromwell was for some time in correspondence with the Duke of Cleves, and as he knew he had a sister, a fair lady, he thought to make a match between her and the King, so he presently sent one of his gentlemen, named Philip Hoby, with letters to the Duke of Cleves, and orders to bring back a painting of the Duke's sister. In a short time Philip Hoby arrived there, and was received by the Duke with much distinction; and after reading the letters he brought, his errand was soon put into effect, and a good painter was obtained who produced a portrait of the lady. The Duke wrote back to the Secretary by Philip Hoby; and when Cromwell saw the portrait, and found the lady was pretty, he was very glad. One day, when he noticed that the King was very merry, he drew him apart, and said, 'May it please your Majesty, I want to show you the portrait of a very pretty lady.'

To which the King replied, 'I should like to see it.' So it was brought, and as soon as the King saw it he asked who the lady was, and Cromwell replied, 'May it please your Majesty, she is the sister of the Duke of Cleves, and is called Madam Anne of Cleves.'

Then the King said, 'Yes, she seems by her dress as if she came from those parts.'

And the Secretary added, 'If your Majesty were to marry again she would suit you.'

The King liked the idea, and said, 'Come hither, Cromwell; how is it you have this portrait here?'

And Cromwell said, 'May it please your Majesty, I sent expressly for it, and if she had not been handsome I would not have shown it to your Majesty.'

'Well,' said the King, 'I will send thither, and if I see she will suit me I will ask for her.'

Cromwell, when he heard what the King said, was delighted, and secretly dispatched a courier to the Duke to advise him of what was going on...

The King was advised of her coming, and she then started on the road to London, spending six days in the journey. On New Year's Day the King set out to receive her, as we will tell.

Cromwell's pleasure cannot be described at having arranged this match, although it turned out wrong for him, as will be told.

CHAPTER XLII

HOW THIS LADY WAS RECEIVED, AND THE GREAT EXPENDI-
TURE THAT CROMWELL CAUSED TO BE MADE.

Very recently Cromwell had prevailed upon the King to grant to
the foreigners in London free permission to exercise their customs,
and that they should for a period of seven years pay no more than
Englishmen, and, in order that this lady should have the more bril-
liant reception, he sent for the principal men of the various nations
in London, and said to them, 'Gentlemen, I wish you to show the
love you bear to the King, and gratitude for the boon he has
granted you, by going out and receiving the new Queen with due
honour.'

The foreigners answered, 'My lord, we will confer together, and
will do what we can.' So they went, and they all agreed that on the
day of the reception they would go forth dressed in riding tunics of
velvet, each man with a servant well appointed, and that they should
all wear red caps with white feathers. They all arranged to adopt this
garb, except the Germans, who were dressed differently.

Then Cromwell sent for the Mayor of London and all the
Aldermen and the Trade Guilds, and caused them to sally forth as
well; in short, there were doubtless over three thousand horses, and it
was a pretty sight to see the devices and bravery that the citizens
wore.

On New Year's Day, at eight o'clock, they left London for Greenwich, three miles off; and above Greenwich there was a field, more
than three miles in extent, where Cromwell had them all placed in
order, some on one side and some on the other, like a lane, over three
miles long; and Cromwell himself looked more like a post-runner
than anything else, running up and down with his staff in his hand.

The lady was late in arriving at Greenwich, for it was nearly four
in the afternoon when she came. It was much noticed that the King
came along with her, but showed in his face that he was disap-

pointed. It was said that he had stayed with her at Rochester, and, it is believed, found her not to his liking.

When they arrived at Greenwich, the ships and the town let off so much artillery, that it was fearful; and all the citizens and foreigners returned to the city, and the next morning the Archbishop said mass, and married the King.

This Madam of Cleves always paid great honour to Madam Mary; and it was noticed that from that day forward the King was not so gay as usual, and presently he did what will be told.

CHAPTER XLIII

HOW THE KING SENT A GENTLEMAN TO CLEVES, AND HOW HE LEARNT THAT THE LADY WAS ALREADY MARRIED.

As the King was discontented with this marriage, he secretly called one of his gentlemen, named Vaughan, and said to him, 'Vaughan, you will go to Cleves, and when you are there pretend you are on your way to Germany. I will supply you with plenty of money, and you will try to find out what you can there, and, particularly, whether this wife of mine had been married before; but do it so that nobody may know the object of your journey. Vaughan departed; and on his arrival at Cleves visited the Duke, who gave him very good cheer, and asked him whither he was going; to which Vaughan replied that he was on his way to Germany, but that he desired to come to Cleves and salute the Duke.

By the time he had been there three days he got very friendly with the Duke's knights and gentlemen, and invited a good many of them to a feast, where they got drunk, and one of them said, 'Master Vaughan, how does the King get on with the sister of the Duke?'

'Very well, master,' said Vaughan; and then this gentleman retorted, 'The Duke greatly wronged a knight who was married to her, and who not a month ago died of grief in Germany, when he learnt that the Duke had taken her away from him to give to the King.'

When Vaughan heard this he dissembled for the time, but the next day he took the gentleman aside, and said to him, 'sir, pray tell me how it was the Duke took Mistress Anne away from her husband?' and the gentleman answered, 'You know that at the time Secretary Cromwell spoke to the Duke about the marriage he sent the husband of the lady to Germany without anyone knowing anything about it, and when we learnt of the King's marriage we were astounded, but the Duke ordered us all expressly not to dare to write a word to the gentleman, her husband. There was no lack of people to let him know, however, after the lady was gone, and when he heard of it he was so grieved that he died.'

Then said Vaughan, 'sir, if you would like to go to England I will undertake to get you very good wages from the King, my master, and I wish that you would give me a letter for him, for he will be glad to hear all this.'

This gentleman was a relative of the one who had died, and answered, 'Master Vaughan, whenever the King wishes to know about it, there are many with the Duke who are well aware of it, but I will write to the King on the subject willingly.' Vaughan asked him what was the gentleman's name, and he told him, but as I do not know it, I do not put it here; and Vaughan then went off, pretending to go to Germany, but really returned to the King, and told him what had passed.

The King at once wrote to the gentleman, promising him great things, and begging him to advise him fuUy as to what had taken place; and the post soon arrived at Cleves, and the letter was delivered to the gentleman, who by return informed the King of everything that had happened, and assured him that if it were necessary he could have it confirmed by the signatures of many gentlemen.

When the King received this information he could not restrain himself from summoning the Queen, to whom he said, 'Madam, I wish to know the truth about one thing, and I promise you on my honour that if you tell me I will deal with you in a way that will please you.' Then he asked her to tell him how long she had been married to the gentleman, and whether he was still alive when she married the King, to which she replied, 'Please your Majesty, it is true I was espoused to him, but when the Duke spoke to me about marrying your Majesty, he told me my husband was dead, and I know nothing more about it.'

Then the King sent the Duke a very angry letter, saying he was astonished that he should have given him somebody else's wife to marry, particularly as he knew he had left Queen Katharine because she had been married to his brother; and he told him, moreover, that henceforward Anne should be no wife of his. When the Duke heard that the King had found it out, he suspected Vaughan had come to inquire, and thought to excuse himself by saying it was not true; but as the gentleman wrote to the King what was going on, and the King sent a detailed account of everything, the Duke saw that he knew all about it, and he could find no excuse, so he wrote saying that his Majesty need not be surprised, as he [the Duke] was obliged to consider his sister's advancement, and informed him that the gentleman was dead, and the King might well remain married to her now.'

When the King received this letter, he sent for Cromwell, and said to him, 'Why hast thou led me into such a great sin as to cause the death of a gentleman? If thou didst know that Anne of Cleves was married, why didst thou make me marry her?'

The Secretary knew what had happened, and God knows how grieved he was that the King should push the matter so far; and he determined to take a very bold course, and said, 'Please your Majesty, I know nothing more than what the Duke wrote me, and your Majesty can see the letters.'

'Well,' said the King, 'let me see them.' There was nothing in them that gave the King any cause for complaint against Cromwell, who stood his ground, and said, 'Your Majesty might well keep her as her first husband is dead; and besides, if your Majesty leaves her, everybody will be saying what a many wives you have.'

He flew into a rage at this, and angrily ordered him out of his presence, and Cromwell went away very crestfallen. The King then sent for the Dukes of Norfolk and Somerset, and said to them, 'I am determined to get rid of Anne of Cleves, and Cromwell shall not deceive me again.'

The Duke of Norfolk was always on bad terms with this secretary, and when he saw the King was angry with him he spoke to the Duke of Somerset, and said, 'Duke, this is the time for us to get rid of common people from our midst; you see that the King has quarrelled with Cromwell, and asks our counsel. We will advise him to take affairs into his own hands, and not be ruled so much by Cromwell.'

This will be related presently; but here I will say that the King made up his mind to leave his wife, and the Dukes of Norfolk and Somerset told him he would be acting wisely, as she was already espoused when the King married her.

CHAPTER XLV

HOW CROMWELL WAS ARRESTED, AND WHAT HE WAS ACCUSED OF.

When the Dukes of Norfolk and Somerset saw the King was angry with Cromwell, they resolved to speak to the King together. The Duke of Somerset, being uncle of the Prince, spoke first, and said, 'May it please your Majesty, all the nobles of the realm are surprised that your Majesty should give so much power to the Secretary, who, doubtless, received a large sum from the Duke of Cleves for bringing about your marriage as he did. Your Majesty might in future take counsel more often with those of your blood, and those who have at heart your Majesty's honour; and if it be true that the Secretary took the bribe, he is deserving of heavy punishment.'

Then the Duke of Norfolk spoke, and said, 'sir, your Majesty will act as you deign to decide; we are only your subjects; but it appears to us that Cromwell's intentions are not good. May it please your Majesty, none of us, however high we may be in the State, have so many servants as he has, and I can prove that in all parts of the kingdom people are wearing his livery and calling themselves his servants, under shelter of which they are committing a thousand offences.'

Then the Marquis of Exeter, who was present at the conference, said, 'Well, I know that he has arms in his house for more than seven thousand men, and we do not like the look of it. Saving your Majesty's presence, moreover, he pays us no respect, and we cannot help noticing that he has put into your Majesty's guard fully forty men who have been his servants, and in your Majesty's chamber there are five devoted servants of his, and many things have been seen and spoken about which convince me that, as things are going, he could do just as he liked, and carry it out successfully. Your Majesty surely should not allow him to take such a stand as would enable him to do anything serious.'

The King, as he was offended with Cromwell, and these lords spoke so affectionately, said, 'My lords, I beeeech you to put up with it for the present, and I promise you I will find a way to take his power away from him.'

These Dukes then communicated with the other lords of the Council, and a gentleman said to the Duke of Somerset, 'May it please your lordship, I was dining with the Emperor's Ambassador a few days since, the Secretary Cromwell being present, and whilst speaking of kings and princes, he said in the hearing of everybody, 'I hope to be a king myself some day;' and added presently, 'I know the Emperor will go to Constantinople and will give me a kingdom.'

'When the Duke heard this he went to the Duke of Norfolk and told him, and they went together to the King and informed him, and the King said, 'My lord Dukes, I desire you tomorrow, as you come out of Parliament after dinner, to order the captain of the guard to secretly arrest him and take him to the Tower, and let it be done without anyone else knowing of it, and I will go and dine with the Bishop of Winchester. I may inform you that I greatly suspect him [Cromwell] of a design to raise the kingdom and murder me, for only a few days ago he had the effrontery to ask me for my daughter Mary for his wife;' to which the Dukes replied, 'Great temerity indeed! and your Majesty should punish him for it.'

'Do as I order now,' said the King, 'and afterwards we will see. If he deserves death he shall suffer it.' Then he commanded that after they had arrested him they should go to his house and take charge of whatever they found there.

The lords were nothing loth. And the next day they all went to Parliament. The Duke of Norfolk, speaking privately to the captain of the guard, told him to secretly arrest the Secretary after dinner, as they were going into the Council, and to take him to the Tower. The captain wondered very much at this, but the Duke said to him, 'You need not be surprised. The King orders it.'

As usual, they all went to the Parliament at Westminster, and when they came out and were going to the palace to dinner, the wind blew off the Secretary's bonnet, and it fell on the ground [compare this story with de Marillac's, Chapter Chapter 13]. The custom of the country is, when a gentleman loses his bonnet, for all those who are with him to doff theirs, but on this occasion, when Cromwell's bonnet blew off, all the other gentlemen kept theirs on their heads, which being noticed by him, he said, 'A high wind indeed must it have been to blow my bonnet off and keep all yours on.' They pretended not to hear what he said, and Cromwell took it for a bad omen. They went to the palace and dined, and all the while they were dining the gentlemen did not converse with the Secretary, as they were wont to do, and as soon as they had finished all the gentlemen went to the Council-chamber. It was the Secretary's habit always after dinner to go close up to a window to hear the petitioners; and when the gentlemen had gone to the Council-chamber, the Secretary remained at his window as usual for about an hour, and then joined the other gentlemen; and finding them all seated, he said, 'You were in a great hurry, gentlemen, to get seated.'

The chair where he was in the habit of sitting was vacant, and the gentlemen made no answer to his remark; but just as he was going to sit down the Duke of Norfolk said, 'Cromwell, do not sit there; that is no place for thee. Traitors do not sit amongst gentlemen.'

He answered, 'I am not a traitor;' and with that the captain of the guard came in and took him by the arm, and said, 'I arrest you.'

'What for?' said he. 'That you will learn elsewhere,' answered the captain. He then asked to see the King, as he wished to speak with him; and he was told that it was not the time now, and was reminded that it was he who passed the law. God's judgment! for he was the first to enact that the King should speak to no one who was accused of treason.

Then the Duke of Norfolk rose and said, 'stop, captain; traitors must not wear the Garter,' and he took it off of him; and then six halberdiers took him by a back door to a boat which the captain had waiting, and he was carried to the Tower; and the Council sent a gentleman, who was said to be Knyvett, to go to his [Cromwell's] house, with fifty halberdiers, and take an inventory of everything they might find, and hold it for the King.

When this gentleman went to Cromwell's house, there were more than three hundred servants waiting at 'Westminster for their master to come out from the Council, and as they saw he was late, and Knyvett was already in the house, they were told to go away, for their master was lodged in the Tower. The poor servants, when they heard this, went home to the house, and when they arrived there, and found the King's halberdiers at the door, their grief may well be imagined.

The King was very kind to them, for he not only ordered them to be given what belonged to them, but commanded the gentlemen to choose servants from amongst them; and he himself took many of them into his service to save them from want.

It soon became known that the Secretary was a prisoner, and from that hour nobody dared to wear his livery or call himself his servant. Formerly there had been over fifteen hundred in the country wearing his livery, and a man thought himself fortunate if he could call himself a servant of Cromwell.

The King sent the principal men of his Council to the Tower to examine the prisoner, and the Duke of Suffolk was the first to speak, saying, 'Cromwell, thou mayst well blame thyself and thy pride for bringing thee to this pass. Say, Cromwell, was it not enough for thee, a blacksmith's son, to have risen to lord it over the whole realm, and to have all of us to do thy bidding, but that the devil must needs put it into thy head and furnish thee with such impudence as to presume to ask the King for the hand of his daughter, who for her goodness deserves the greatest prince in the world? High, indeed, didst thou aspire, and nothing else can be believed but thou didst aim at usurpation of the realm, and to make thyself king, for so didst thou say one day at the Ambassador's. Oh, ignorant ingrate, dost thou not know that if the Emperor won kingdoms he has vassals far more worthy than thou; and besides, what service hast thou rendered to the Emperor that he should make a king of thee? By my faith! it is easier to believe, as we have said, that, if thou couldst have got Madam Mary, thou couldst easily have dispatched the King, for which purpose thou hadst surrounded him with thy creatures, the better to ensure thy fell design; but, since it is all known now, it is no use for thee to try excuses, and it will be better for thee to tell the truth at once, and thank God that the King has commanded that thou shalt not be put to torture, for, if he had not so ordered, such a torture should be given to thee as for many a long day has been given to no one.'

Then all the gentlemen began to talk, and everyone said to him what he liked - very abusive words - to all of which Cromwell answered as follows.

CHAPTER XLVI

HOW CROMWELL AN8WEBED, AND IT WAS KNOWN THAT HE HAD WANTED TO KILL THE DUKE OF NORFOLK.

Cromwell, when he heard the abuse they showered upon him, seeing he could not escape, spoke as follows: 'Duke, if I had carried into effect what I intended once, you would not be ill-treating me now.'

And, that you should know what he meant by this, I will tell you that once Cromwell had arrested a gentleman, a relative of the Duke of Norfolk, accused of high treason, and when he was a prisoner in the Tower, Cromwell went to him, and said, 'Master Dartnall,' for that was his name, 'if thou wilt say that the Duke ordered thee to do what thou. art accused of doing, I will promise to save thy life, and give thee a great revenue.'

Dartnall was accused of attempting to give poison to the Prince, and it was said, that as Cromwell wished to injure the Duke of Norfolk, that was the reason he had Dartnall arrested, hoping, by threats, to get him to say that the Duke had prompted him; but this gentleman would never say it, but answered Cromwell in this fashion: 'Oh! Secretary, I should be the blackest traitor in the world, and there were never traitors in my lineage! Cease thy efforts, then, for I would rather die, and I hope to God that it may never be in thy power to harm him, but I hope to see the day when God may punish thee.'

When they took Cromwell this Dartnall was still in the Tower, and as he was a relative of the Duke, they had not yet put him to torture to make him confess the crime of which they accused him, but the Duke had asked the King to keep him imprisoned, so that in time they would be able to discover the truth. So now the Duke had Dartnall brought there, and before them all he told what we have just related; and, turning to Cromwell, he said, 'Now I shall be revenged on thee for keeping me here all this time, for God has heard my prayer.'

The gentlemen said, even if he had nothing more than this he deserved death; and then Cromwell cried, 'Do not take the trouble, my lords, to find out any more. It is my own fault for not revenging myself upon some of you. Let the King do as he likes with me, for I deserve to die; my only sorrow is that I did not see the death of some of you first.'

The gentlemen ordered Dartnall to be released, and then went to the King and told him what had passed, and the King commanded that Cromwell should immediately be beheaded. We shall speak of him presently, and will now go on to tell what happened afterwards.

CHAPTER XLVII

HOW THE ARCHBISHOP OF CANTERBURY WAS WARNED
THAT HE WAS TO BE ARRESTED, AND HOW HE WENT AT
ONCE TO THE KING, AND WAS PARDONED.

As soon as Cromwell was arrested, it was rumoured that the
Archbishop of Canterbury was to be sent to the Tower; and a
gentleman who was much attached to him went and said to him, 'My
lord Archbishop, how is it you are not providing for your safety? if
you do not promptly find a remedy the King will send you to the
Tower.'

The Archbishop at once asked for his boat, and went straight to
the palace and entered the King's chamber, and knelt before the King,
who asked him, 'What do you come for. Bishop?' to which the Bishop
replied, 'sir, I come to ask your Majesty's pardon, if in anything I have
offended you.'

'Bishop,' said the King, 'they complain to me here that you have
published a book in which there is much heresy, and if this be so, I
shall be very sorry.'

The Bishop answered, 'sir, it is true; and thank God Secretary
Cromwell is alive, who ordered, in your Majesty's name, to have it
preached in all the parishes, which God knows I did against my will.'
I will not say here what the heresy was which was ordered to be
preached, in order to avoid scandal. Then said the King, 'You can go
home. Bishop; I can well believe it is some of Cromwell's work, and
you shall not be punished.'

This Bishop always tried to please the King, and the next day he
and the Duke were ordered to go and tell Cromwell, in the Tower,
that he had to die the day after.

So they went; and the Bishop, in order that the Duke might know
that he had not been to blame, said to Cromwell, 'I beg you to tell me
how many days ago is it since you sent to tell me to have such-and-
such a thing preached and published in books?'

Cromwell answered, 'My lord Bishop, it may be about two months, and it is quite true that I ordered it.'

'Oh, Cromwell,' said the Duke, 'I am sure it is God's will that you should live no longer. It seems you learnt well from the Cardinal, and we have now to tell you that tomorrow you lose your head.'

Then said Cromwell, 'Do all the evil thou canst; but I tell thee, a day will come when you will hold as good that which I ordered to be preached.'

'That day thou wilt not live to see,' said the Duke. It seemed that Cromwell was a prophet, for the heresies got very much worse afterwards, and I pray to our Lord that He may find a remedy, so that so many souls may not perish.

After the Bishop and the Duke had gone, Cromwell remained very pensive all that night. When they got to the King they told him all that Cromwell had said, and from that hour forward the King always had more affection for that bishop. Orders were given that all these books should be burnt, and if any were found in possession of any one the person should be punished. Many were burnt, but not all, as it turned out, for they were not so eager to burn them as they afterwards were to reprint them, although not in the King's lifetime, but under the rule of the Protector.

CHAPTER XLVIII

HOW CROMWELL WAS BEHEADED, AND WHAT HE SAID ON THE SCAFFOLD

The day after the Duke told Cromwell he had to die, the Sheriffs of London were ordered to go to the Tower and bring him out for execution. They went, and he was brought forth with a thousand halberdiers, as a revolt was feared; and if all those who formerly wore his livery and called themselves his servants had been there, they might easily have raised the city, so beloved was he by the common people.

When he was at the scaffold, and had mounted it, he turned to the people, and said, 'Good people, I beseech you pray to God for me.' Then seeing a great many courtiers there, he said to them, 'Gentlemen, you should all take warning from me, who was, as you know, from a poor man made by the King into a great gentleman, and I, not contented with that, nor with having the kingdom at my orders, presumed to a still higher state, and my pride has brought its punishment. I confess I am justly condemned, and I urge you, gentlemen, study to preserve the good you possess, and never let greed or pride prevail in you. Serve your King, who is one of the best in the world, and one who knows best how to reward his vassals.'

Amongst all these gentlemen he noticed Master Wyatt, the gentleman who had been imprisoned for the affair of Queen Anne; and he called him, and said, 'Oh, gentle Wyatt, goodbye, and pray to God for me.' There was always great friendship between these two, and Wyatt could not answer him for tears.

All these gentlemen marvelled greatly to see that Master Wyatt was in such grief, and Cromwell, who was a very clever man, noticing it, said out loud, 'Oh, Wyatt, do not weep, for if I were no more guilty than thou wert when they took thee, I should not be in this pass.' Everybody was very fond of Wyatt, so they pretended not to notice; but if it had been anyone else they might have arrested him, to see whether he knew of any other treason which Cromwell might have plotted.

When these words were ended, he turned round to the scaffold, and seeing the headsman ready, he said, 'Pray, if possible, cut off the head with one blow, so that I may not suffer much.' Then the headsman asked his pardon, and Cromwell knelt, and laid his head on the block, and the headsman succeeded in striking off the head with a single stroke of the axe. And so ended this Cromwell, who had better never have been born, for he was the inventor of all the bad sects which they have now.

BANDELLO'S NOVELLE (1554)

Matteo Bandello (*c.*1480 – 1562) was an Italian writer, soldier, monk, and later, a bishop. He wrote a number of poems, but his fame rests entirely on his extensive collection of *Novelle*, or tales (1554, 1573). Shakespeare's Much Ado about Nothing, Romeo and Juliet and Twelfth Night are believed to be based in sources derived from Bandello's works. In the *novella* extract below, Bandello tells a story of Thomas Cromwell's travels in Italy and his friendship with the banker Francesco Frescobaldi.

There was at Florence, not many years since, a man named Francesco, of the ancient and noble family of the Frescobaldi and a very loyal and honourable merchant, who, according to the usance of the country, although very rich, trafficked in various parts and carried on a great business. He sojourned well-nigh always in England and had his residence in London, where he lived very splendidly and practised great hospitality, not looking so closely to it as do many merchants, who look to the least farthing, Ansaldo Grimaldi of Genoa to wit, who, I understand, keepeth count even of the least sheet of paper and of an end of twine for tying packets of letters. It chanced one day that, Francesco Frescobaldi being in Florence, a poor man presented himself before him and craved him charity for the love of God. Frescobaldo, seeing him so ill accoutred and noting signs of gentle breeding in his countenance, was moved to pity, more by token that he knew him to be English; and accordingly he asked him what countryman he was.

He answered that he was English and Frescobaldo asking him divers particulars concerning England, as one who was thoroughly conversant therewith, the young man very aptly satisfied him of the whole, saying, 'I am called Thomas Cromwell and am the son of a poor clothdresser. I fled away from my father and coming to Italy with the French army, which was routed at Il Garigliano, abode with a footsoldier, after whom I carried the pike.'

Frescobaldo carried him home to his house and there very hospitably entertained him some days for the love of the English nation, from whom he had received many kindnesses, clothing him and entreating him kindly; moreover, when he was minded to depart and return to his native country, he gave him sixteen gold ducats in Florentine money and a good hackney.

The young man, seeing himself so well furnished, returned Frescobaldo such best thanks as he might and betook himself home to England. Now he knew, according to the excellent usance of wellnigh all the Ultramontanes [i.e. the non-Italians], to read and wrote very aptly after the English fashion. He was a youth of exceeding high spirit, quick-witted and prompt of resolution, knowing excellent well to accommodate himself to the wishes of others, and could, whenas seemed to him to the purpose, dissemble his passions better than any man in the world. Moreover, he endured all bodily fatigue with patience, so that, having engaged for counsellor with the Cardinal of York [i.e. Wolsey], a prelate of very great authority, he in a little while grew to great repute with him and was much employed by him in all his affairs.

The cardinal was then in exceeding credit with the English king and governed the whole island, holding a court so great and so worshipful that it had sufficed a most puissant prince; whence it befell that he oftentimes sent Cromwell to speak with the king of affairs of the utmost moment and the young man knew so well to ingratiate himself with the latter that he began to show him a good countenance, seeming to himself he was a man apt to the manage of whatsoever most important business. Now the king, with the cardinal's connivance, had then late repudiated Catherine his wife, daughter of Ferdinand the Catholic, King of Spain, and mother's sister of the Emperor Charles of Austria, in the expectation that the pope would confirm the writ of repudiation and dissolve the marriage, for the reasons assigned by him; but the pope, accounting the repudiation unlawful, would not confirm it; wherefore the cardinal fell into disgrace with the king and was dismissed the court.

After his departure from court, the cardinal reduced his household, keeping but a small number of folk about him, and daily rid him of one servant or another; wherefore the king, remembering him of Cromwell, who had aforetime given him such satisfaction, let summon him and said to him, 'Cromwell, as thou seest, the cardinal hath retired [from office] and hath no longer need for so many servants as when he managed the affairs of my kingdom; and thou art presently out of employ, having nothing to treat for him. Hast thou a mind to serve me?'

'Sire,' replied the other, 'I have still served the cardinal very faithfully and will do the like with yourself, an you deign to avail yourself of me.'

'It is well,' rejoined the king; 'even so would I have thee do, for that such is the expectation I have of thy dealings.'

With this he made him his principal secretary, employing him in whatsoever occasions of importance betided him; wherein he bore him so well that the king gave him his privy seal in keeping and there were few in the kingdom had such influence with him as Cromwell, who to his mind was worth all those at court. Moreover, it seeming to that blind trull Fortune that she had not done enough in raising Cromwell from the earth and uplifting him to such a height, she must needs exalt him yet higher; wherefore she caused the king create him Constable of the realm, an office which none other may be evened, under the kingship. [Note: Cromwell was never Constable of

England, for the simple reason that Henry VIII himself abolished the office of Lord High Constable in the early part of his reign, long before he took Cromwell into his service; the highest dignity conferred upon Cromwell was that of Lord Chamberlain of England, which is probably that meant hy Bandello or his informant.]

Having made him Constable, the king gave all the governance of the realm into his hand and so Cromwell came to such a height that it was a thing incredible. Being grown to such a pitch of greatness, he showed himself a bitter enemy unto all the nobility of the island; nay, whenassoever he might avail to do some gentleman a mischief, he failed not thereof, and if the king took a spite against any of them, he still added fuel to the fire.

Meanwhile, the king determined (his wife, Catherine of Spain, being yet alive,) to take another wife at all risks and unable at any price to obtain the pope's dispensation, he dispensed withal for himself; whence there arose infinite disorders in the kingdom of England and it became altogether severed from the Holy Catholic Mother Church of Rome, on such wise that innumerable monks and friars, refusing to consent to that his pleasure, were beheaded and many gentlemen and barons put to death. Many prelates and others of very godly life were also beheaded and matters came to such a pitch that few days passed but some one's head was smitten off and the nobility of England became well-nigh extinguished, the nobles being much more rigorously persecuted than men of low degree. Of all these ills Cromwell was generally believed to be the instigator, inasmuch as he hated the nobility beyond measure and sought to have it altogether extinguished, knowing himself begotten of very mean blood. But I purpose not for the nonce to recount to you the heinous and unrighteous cruelties and butcheries which were at that time done in England; nay, I began this story, to relate to you that which betided Frescobaldo of the hospitality shown by him to Cromwell.

You must know, then, that, in the days when Cromwell was master

and governor of the island, Francesco Frescobaldi chanced to be in
Italy, where, having, as often happeneth to merchants, suffered many
disasters and great losses of his merchandise, he became very poor;
for that, being a loyal and worthy man, he paid all to whom he was
indebted and could not recover that which was owed him of others.
Finding himself reduced to such poor estate, he cast up his accounts
and found that he had more than fifteen thousand ducats owing him
in England; wherefore he determined to betake himself thither and
apply to recover the most that should be possible, purposing to pass
the rest of his life in quiet. Accordingly he passed over from Italy into
France and from France into England and took up his abode in
London, remembering him not withal of the kindness which he had
erst done Cromwell in Florence; a thing in sooth worthy of a truly
liberal man, who keepeth no account of the courtesies he doth others,
but graveth in marble those which he receiveth, so he may repay
them whenassoever the occasion offereth itself to him. He busied
himself, therefore, in London with the transaction of his affairs and
as he went one day through a certain street, it befell that the
constable himself passed through the same street from an opposite
direction. No sooner did he set eyes upon Frescobaldo's face than he
remembered him to be certainly he of whom he had received such
courtesy in Florence; wherefore, being a-horseback, he dismounted
and to the exceeding wonderment of those who were with him, (for
that there were more than an hundred mounted men in his train of
the chiefest of the kingdom,) he embraced him very lovingly and said
to him, well-nigh weeping, 'Are you not Francesco Frescobaldi of
Florence?'

'Ay am I, my lord,' replied the other, 'and your humble servant.'

'My servant!' cried the constable. 'That are you not nor will I have
you for such, but for my dear friend. Nay, I must tell you that I have
just reason to complain sore of you, for that you, knowing who I am
and where I was, should have let me know your coming hither, so I
might have paid some part of the debt in which I confess myself
beholden to you. Now God be thanked that I am yet in time! You are
very welcome. I go presently upon the king my master's affairs and

can make no longer stay with you; wherefore do you hold me excused, but look you come dine with me this morning and that without fail.'

And therewithal he remounted to horse and repaired to the king at court.

Frescobaldo, the constable gone, remembered him that this was the young Englishman whom he had aforetime harboured in his house at Florence and began to be of good hope, bethinking him that the interest of so great a man would much avail him in the recoverance of his monies. Accordingly, at dinner-time, he betook himself to the constable's palace and waited but a little while in the courtyard ere he returned. As soon as he was dismounted, he embraced Frescobaldo anew on friendly wise and turning to the [Lord High] Admiral and other princes and gentlemen who were come to dine with him, 'Sirs,' said he, 'marvel not at the love which I show this Florentine gentleman, for that this is in payment of infinite obligations in which I acknowledge myself beholden to him, it being by his means that I am in my present rank; and you shall hear how.'

Then, in presence of all, still holding the Florentine by the hand, he told them how he had arrived at Florence and the kindnesses he had received from Frescobaldo; and so they mounted the stairs and entering the saloon, sat down to table. The constable would have Frescobaldo sit beside himself and still entreated him most lovingly.

When they had dined and the guests had departed, he desired to know the occasion of Frescobaldo's return to London; whereupon the latter related to him the whole story of his mischances and how, there being left him, beyond his house in Florence and an estate in the country, well-nigh nothing save those fifteen thousand ducats which were owed him in England, (and belike some two thousand in Spain,) he had betaken himself to that island to recover them.

'It is well,' said the constable. 'As for things past, they may not anywise be undone; I can indeed condole with you of your misfortunes, as I do with all my heart. For the rest I will take such order that you shall recover all the monies which arc owing to you here, nor shall you lack aught of that which is in my power, for I assure you that the courtesy you showed me, whenas you had no knowledge of me, rendereth me so much beholden to you that I shall still be yours and you may dispose of me and mine as if you were myself. The which an you do not, the loss will be your own, nor do I make you any farther proffer, meseeming it were superfluous. Suffice it that this be said to you once for all. But now let us arise and go to my chamber.'

[Accordingly they went thither], where the constable, shutting the door, opened a great coffer of ducats and taking sixteen thereof, gave them to Frescobaldo, saying, 'Here, my friend, are the sixteen ducats you gave me on my departure from Florence and here other ten which the hackney cost you, which you bought for me, and yet other ten, which you spent in clothing me. But since you are a merchant and meseemeth fair and right that your monies should not have lain so long dead, but should have profited, each of which are four thousand ducats. Do you take them in return for yours and enjoy them for the love of me.'

Frescobaldo, albeit he had fallen from great wealth to great poverty, had withal not lost his generosity of mind and would not accept the sixteen thousand ducats, thanking the constable none the less for that his great courtesy; but in the end, constrained by Cromwell, he must perforce take them and the constable would eke have him give him a note of the names of all his debtors; to which he very willingly consented and set down the same in writing, together with the sums which they owed him. Cromwell thereupon called a man of his household and said to him, 'Look who these be that are set down in this schedule and see thou find them all out, be they where they may in this island, and give them to understand that, except they pay their whole debt within fifteen days' time, I will put my hand to the matter, and that to their hurt and displeasance; wherefore let them consider that I am their creditor.'

The man did his master's commandment very diligently, so that by the appointed term there were some fifteen thousand ducats recovered; nay, had Frescobaldo required the interest which had run in so long a time, he had had it to the uttermost farthing; but he contented himself with the capital and would have no interest whatever; the which gained him exceeding good repute and favour with all, especially as it was already known of the whole island what interest he had with the constable. Meanwhile he was the constant guest of the latter, who daily studied to honour him as most he might and for that he would fain have had him constantly abide in London, his converse much pleasing him, he proffered him the loan of three-score thousand ducats for four years, so he might set lip a house and bank in London and trade withal; nor did he require aught of profit usance therefor and he promised him, to boot, every possible favour in matters of merchandry. But Frescobaldo, being desirous of returning home and passing the rest of his life in ease and quiet, thanked him infinitely for such exceeding courtesy and remitting all his monies to Florence, returned, with the constable's good leave, to his native place, where, being now rich enough, he applied himself to live a very quiet life; this, however, he enjoyed but a little while, inasmuch as he died that same year at Florence.

What shall we say, now, of Cromwell's gratitude and liberality? Certes, as to that which he did with Frescobaldo, meseemeth it was worthy of the utmost commendation; and had he loved the nobility of his country as he seemed to love foreigners, belike he had been yet alive; but he hated the English nobles overmuch and this in the end was the cause of his death. Nay, since there is no otherwhat to say, I will e'en tell you how he died. He abode some years in favour with the king and blinded by fair fortune, was mighty ready at letting cut off this and the other's head; nay, the nobler and greater they were, the fainer was he to show his power over them, whether they were churchmen or laymen. Now it befell that, thinking to have the Bishop of Winchester put to death (for what reason I know not) and being in the king's privy council, he bade the prelate in question render himself the king's prisoner at the Tower, a place where, according to that which is said of the people of the country, none ever entered but he was slain. The bishop, aghast at such a commandment, replied that he knew not what cause he had given to be thus entreated and that he would first speak with the king. 'That can you not,' replied the constable; 'get you gone whither I tell you,' and bade four of his men hale him off to prison. What while they were a-wrangling, the Duke of Suffolk, who was Cromwell's enemy, went to speak with the king in an adjoining chamber and told him of the contention between the constable and the bishop. The king, who knew nothing of the matter, sent one of his gentlemen of the chamber to call the bishop; which the constable, hearing, was sore despited and going home, abode four days without showing himself at court or at the counciltable. The bishop accordingly presented himself before the king and declared that he knew not in what he had offended, but that he was in the king's hand, who should let do justice upon him, if he had made default. The king, seeing that Cromwell appeared not at court and that nothing was found against the bishop, released him, saying, in the hearing of the whole court, 'I will e'en see who best knoweth to keep his choler, I who am king or Thomas Cromwell.'

Meanwhile, he being known to be angered, many complaints were presented to him against the constable and it was found that he had been guilty of many misdeeds, especially in matters of law and justice. At the end of the four days, the constable repaired to the privy council and the place of assembly being shut, the king sent a councillor to bid Cromwell's retinue go dine and after return, for that their lord dined that morning with the king. Accordingly, they all went away and the king sending for his archers, posted them before the door of the council-chamber. The council ended, the constable came out and was taken by the archers and told that he was the king's prisoner; then, being carried to the Tower, he was there kept in strict custody, whilst his trial was set afoot, and a few days thereafterward his head was, by the king's commandment, smitten off in the Castle Green. Now, had he known to put a [nail] in Fortune's wheel, that is to say, to live as a gentleman and not be so greedy of human blood, his end had belike been a better and a more honourable.

CAVENDISH'S LIFE OF WOLSEY (1554–8)

George Cavendish (1497–c.1562) was the biographer of Cardinal Thomas Wolsey, whose *Thomas Wolsey, Late Cardinall, his Lyffe and Deathe* is the major contemporary source for Wolsey's life – he was a 'gentleman-she' in Wolsey's service from 1522 to 1530. Here he begins by describing a scene in Wolsey's household in 1529, and then another in 1530 – by this time Wolsey had been accused of treason and was stripped of his property; suffering from failing health, he died in November 1530 while travelling to Yorkshire.

It chanced me upon All-hallown day to come there into the Great Chamber at Asher, in the morning, to give mine attendance, where I found Master Cromwell leaning in the great window, with a Primer in his hand, saying of our Lady mattins; which had been since a very strange sight. He prayed not more earnestly than the tears distilled from his eyes. Whom I bade good morrow. And with that I perceived the tears upon his cheeks. To whom I said, 'Why Master Cromwell, what meaneth all this your sorrow? Is my lord in any danger, for whom ye lament thus? or is it for any loss that ye have sustained by any misadventure?'

'Nay, nay,' quoth he, 'it is my unhappy adventure, which am like to

lose all that I have travailed for all the days of my life, for doing of my
master true and diligent service.'

'Why, sir,' quoth I, 'I trust ye be too wise, to commit any thing by
my lord's commandment, otherwise than ye might do of right,
whereof ye have any cause to doubt of loss of your goods.'

'Well, well,' quoth he, 'I cannot tell; but all things I see before
mine eyes, is as it is taken; and this I understand right well, that I am
in disdain with most men for my master's sake; and surely without
just cause. Howbeit, an ill name once gotten will not lightly be put
away. I never had any promotion by my lord to the increase of my
living. And thus much will I say to you, that I intend, God willing, this
afternoon, when my lord hath dined, to ride to London, and so to the
court, where I will either make or mar, or I come again. I will put
myself in prease, to see what any man is able to lay to my charge of
untruth or misdemeanour.'

'Marry, sir,' quoth I, 'in so doing, in my conceit, ye shall do very
well and wisely, beseeching God to be your guide, and send you good
luck, even as I would myself.' And with that I was called into the
closet, to see and prepare all things ready for my lord, who intended
that day to say mass there himself; and so I did.

And then my lord [i.e. Wolsey] came thither with his chaplain,
one Doctor Marshall, saying first his mattins, and heard two masses
on his knees. And then after he was confessed, he himself said mass.
And when he had finished mass, and all his divine service, returned
into his chamber, where he dined among divers of his doctors, where
as Master Cromwell dined also; and sitting at dinner, it chanced that
my lord commended the true and faithful service of his gentlemen
and yeomen. Whereupon Master Cromwell took an occasion to say to
my lord, that in conscience he ought to consider their truth and loyal
service that they did him, in this his present necessity, which never
forsaketh him in all his trouble.

'It shall be well done, therefore,' said he, 'for your grace to call
before you all these your most worthy gentlemen and right honest
yeomen, and let them understand, that ye right well consider their
patience, truth, and faithfulness; and then give them your commen-

dation, with good words and thanks, the which shall be to them great courage to sustain your mishap in patient misery, and to spend their life and substance in your service.'

'Alas, Thomas,' quoth my lord unto him, 'ye know I have nothing to give them, and words without deeds be not often well taken. For if I had but as I have had of late, I would depart with them so frankly as they should be well content: but nothing hath no savour; and I am ashamed, and also sorry that I am not able to requite their faithful service. And although I have cause to rejoice, considering the fidelity I perceive in the number of my servants, who will not depart from me in my miserable estate, but be as diligent, obedient, and serviceable about me as they were in my great triumphant glory, yet do I lament again the want of substance to distribute among them.'

'Why, sir,' quoth Master Cromwell, 'have ye not here a number of chaplains, to whom ye have departed very liberally with spiritual promotions, in so much as some may dispend, by your grace's prefer-ment, a thousand marks by the year, and some five hundred marks, and some more, and some less; ye have no one chaplain within all your house, or belonging unto you, but he may dispend at the least well (by your procurement and preferment) three hundred marks yearly, who had all the profit and advantage at your hands, and other your servants none at all; and yet hath your poor servants taken much more pains for you in one day than all your idle chaplains hath done in a year. Therefore if they will not freely and frankly consider your liberality, and depart with you of the same goods gotten in your service, now in your great indigence and necessity, it is pity that they live; and all the world will have them in indignation and hatred, for their abominable ingratitude to their master and lord.'

'I think no less, Thomas,' quoth my lord, 'wherefore, [I pray you,] cause all my servants to be called and to assemble without, in my great chamber, after dinner, and see them stand in order, and I will declare unto them my mind, according to your advice.'

After that the board's end was taken up, Master Cromwell came to me and said, 'Heard you not, what my Lord said even now?'

'Yes, sir,' quoth I, 'that I did.'

'Well, then,' quoth he, 'assemble all my lord's servants up into the great chamber;' and so I did, and when they were all there assembled, I assigned all the gentlemen to stand on the right side of the chamber, and the yeomen on the left side. And at the last my lord came thither, appareled in a white rochet upon a violet gown of cloth like a bishop's, who went straight into the great window. Standing there a while, and his chaplains about him, beholding the number of his servants divided in two parts, he could not speak unto them for tenderness of his heart; the flood of tears that distilled from his eyes declared no less: the which perceived by his servants, caused the fountains of water to gush out of their faithful hearts down their cheeks, in such abundance as it would cause a cruel heart to lament. At the last, after he had turned his face to the wall, and wiped his eyes with his handkerchief, he spake to them after this sort in effect:

'Most faithful gentlemen and true hearted yeomen, I do not only lament [to see] your persons present about me, but I do lament my negligent ingratitude towards you all on my behalf, in whom hath been a great default, that in my prosperity [I] have not done for you so much as I might have done, either in word or deed, which was then in my power to do: but then I knew not my jewels and special treasures that I had of you my faithful servants in my house; but now approved experience hath taught me, and with the eyes of my discretion, which before were hid, I do perceive well the same...

...if the king do not thus shortly restore me, then will I see you bestowed according to your own requests, and write for you, either to the king, or to any other noble person within this realm, to retain you into service; for I doubt not but the king, or any noble man, or worthy gentleman of this realm, will credit my letter in your commendation... Therefore I desire you to take your pleasures for a month, and then ye may come again unto me, and I trust by that time, the king's majesty will extend his clemency upon me.'

'Sir,' quoth Master Cromwell, 'there is divers of these your yeomen, that would be glad to see their friends, but they lack money: therefore here is divers of your chaplains who have received at your hands great benefices and high dignities; let them therefore now show themselves unto you as they are bound by all humanity to do. I think their honesty and charity is not so slender and void of grace that they would not see you lack where they may help to refresh you. And for my part, although I have not received of your grace's gift one penny towards the increase of my yearly living, yet will I depart with you this towards the dispatch of your servants,' and [therewith] delivered him five pounds in gold.

'And now let us see what your chaplains will do. I think they will depart with you much more than I have done, who be more able to give you a pound than I one penny.'

'Go to, masters,' quoth he to the chaplains: in so much as some gave to him ten pounds, some ten marks, some a hundred shillings, and so some more and some less, as at that time their powers did extend; whereby my lord received among them as much money of their liberality as he gave to each of his yeomen a quarter's wages, and board wages for a month; and they departed down into the hall, where some determined to go to their friends, and some said that they would not depart from my lord until they might see him in better estate. My lord returned into his chamber lamenting the departure from his servants, making his moan unto Master Cromwell, who comforted him the best he could, and desired my lord to give him leave to go to London, where he would either make or mar or he came again, which was always his common saying. Then after long communication with my lord in secret, he departed and took his horse, and rode to London, at whose departing I was by, whom he bade farewell; and said, 'ye shall hear shortly of me, and if I speed well, I will not fail to be here again within these two days.' And so I took my leave of him, and he rode forth on his journey. Sir Rafe Sadler, (now knight), was then his clerk, and rode with him...

Now let us return again to Master Cromwell, to see how he hath sped, since his departure last from my lord. The case stood so, that there should begin, shortly after All-hallown tide, the Parliament, and [he], being within London, devised with himself to be one of the Burgesses of the Parliament, and chanced to meet with one Sir Thomas Rush, knight, a special friend of his, whose son was appointed to be one of the Burgesses of that Parliament, of whom he obtained his room, and by that means put his foot into the Parliament House: then within two or three days after his entry into the Parliament, he came unto my lord, to Asher, with a much pleasanter countenance than he had at his departure, and meeting with me before he came to my lord, said unto me, 'that he had once adventured to put in his foot, where he trusted shortly to be better regarded, or all were done.' And when he was come to my lord, they talked together in secret manner; and that done, he rode out of hand again that night to London, because he would not be absent from the Parliament the next morning. There could nothing be spoken against my lord in the Parliament House but he would answer it incontinent, or else take until the next day, against which time he would resort to my lord to know what answer he should make in his behalf; in so much that there was no matter alleged against my lord but that he was ever ready furnished with a sufficient answer; so that at length, for his honest behaviour in his master's cause, he grew into such estimation in every man's opinion, that he was esteemed to be the most faithfullest servant to his master of all other, wherein he was of all men greatly commended.

Then was there brought in a Bill of Articles into the Parliament House to have my lord condemned of treason; against which bill Master Cromwell inveighed so discreetly, with such witty persuasions and deep reasons, that the same bill could take there no effect.

After this time my lord daily amended, and so continued still at Asher [Esher, not far from Wolsey's former home at Hampton Court] until Candlemas [in February 1530]; against which feast, the king caused to be sent him three or four cart loads of stuff, and most part thereof was locked in great standards, (except beds and kitchen-stuff,) wherein was both plate and rich hangings, and chapel-stuff. Then my lord, being thus furnished, was therewith well contented...

Then commanded he Master Cromwell, being with him, to make

suit to the king's majesty, that he might remove thence to some other place, for he was weary of that house of Asher: for with continual use thereof the house waxed unsavoury; supposing that if he might remove from thence he should much sooner recover his health. And also the council had put into the king's head, that the new gallery at Asher, which my lord had late before his fall newly set up, should be very necessary for the king, to take down and set it up again at Westminster; which was done accordingly, and stands at this present day there. The taking away thereof before my lord's face was to him a corrosive, which was invented by his enemies only to torment him, the which indeed discouraged him very sore to tarry any longer there.

Now Master Cromwell thought it but vain and much folly to move any of the king's council to assist and prefer his suit to the king, among whom rested the number of his mortal enemies, for they would rather hinder his removing, or else remove him farther from the king, than to have holpen him to any place nigh the king's common trade; wherefore he refused any suit to them, and made only suit to the king's own person; whose suit the king graciously heard, and thought it very convenient to be granted; and through the special motion of Master Cromwell, the king was well contented that he should remove to Richmond, which place my lord had a little before repaired to his great cost and charge; for the king had made an exchange thereof with him for Hampton Court. All this his removing was done without the knowledge of the king's council, for if they might have had any intelligence thereof before, then would they have persuaded the king to the contrary: but when they were advertised of the king's grant and pleasure, they dissimuled their countenances in the king's presence, for they were greatly afraid of him, lest his nigh being, the king might at length some one time resort to him, and so call him home again, considering the great affection and love that the king daily showed towards him; wherefore they doubted his rising again, if they found not a mean to remove him shortly from the king. In so much that they thought it convenient for their purpose to inform the king upon certain considerations which they invented, that it were very necessary that my lord should go down into the

North unto his benefice of York, where he should be a good stay for the country; to the which the king, supposing that they had meant no less than good faith, granted and condescended to their suggestions; which were forced so with wonderful imagined considerations, that the king, understanding nothing of their intent, was lightly persuaded to the same. Whereupon the Duke of Norfolk commanded Master Cromwell, who had daily access unto him, to say to my lord, that it is the king's pleasure that he should with speed go to his benefice, where lieth his cure, and look to that according to his duty.

Master Cromwell at his next repair to my lord, who lay then at Richmond, declared unto him what my Lord of Norfolk said, how it was determined that he should go to his benefice.

'Well then, Thomas,' quoth my lord, 'seeing there is no other remedy, I do intend to go to my benefice of Winchester, and I pray you, Thomas, so show my Lord of Norfolk.'

'Contented, sir,' quoth Master Cromwell, and according to his commandment did so.

To the which my Lord of Norfolk answered and said, 'What will he do there?'

'Nay,' quoth he, 'let him go into his province of York, whereof he hath received his honour, and there lieth the spiritual burden and charge of his conscience, as he ought to do, and so show him.'

The lords, who were not all his friends, having intelligence of his intent, thought to withdraw his appetite from Winchester, and would in no wise permit him to plant himself so nigh the king: [they] moved therefore the king to give my lord but a pension out of Winchester, and to distribute all the rest among the nobility and other of his worthy servants; and in likewise to do the same with the revenues of St. Albans; and of the revenues of his colleges in Oxford and Ipswich, the which the king took into his own hands; whereof Master Cromwell had the receipt and government before by my lord's assignment. In consideration thereof it was thought most convenient that he should have so still. Notwithstanding, out of the revenues of Winchester and St. Albans the king gave to some one nobleman three hundred marks, and to some a hundred pounds, and to some more and to some less, according to the king's royal pleasure. Now Master Cromwell executed his office, the which he had over the lands of the college, so justly and exactly that he was had in great estimation for his witty behaviour therein, and also for the true, faithful, and diligent service extended towards my lord his master.

It came at length so to pass that those to whom the king's majesty had given any annuities or fees for term of life by patent out of the forenamed revenues could not be good, but [only] during my lord's life, forasmuch as the king had no longer estate or title therein, which came to him by reason of my lord's attainder in the premunire; and to make their estates good and sufficient according to their patents, it was thought necessary to have my lord's confirmation unto their grants. And this to be brought about, there was no other mean but to make suit to Master Cromwell to obtain their confirmation at my lord's hands, whom they thought might best obtain the same.

Then began both noblemen and other who had any patents of the king, out either of Winchester or St. Albans, to make earnest suit to Master Cromwell for to solicit their causes to my lord, to get of him his confirmations; and for his pains therein sustained, they promised every man, not only worthily to reward him, but also to show him such pleasures as should at all times lie in their several powers, whereof they assured him. Wherein Master Cromwell perceiving an occasion and a time given him to work for himself, and to bring the thing to pass which he long wished for; intended to work so in this matter, to serve their desires, that he might the sooner bring his own enterprise to purpose.

Then at his next resort to my lord, he moved him privily in this matter to have his counsel and his advice, and so by their witty heads it was devised that they should work together by one line, to bring by their policies Master Cromwell in place and estate, where he might do himself good and my lord much profit. Now began matters to work to bring Master Cromwell into estimation in such sort as was afterwards much to his increase of dignity; and thus every man, having an occasion to sue for my lord's confirmation, made now earnest travail to Master Cromwell for these purposes, who refused none to make promise that he would do his best in that case. And having a great occasion of access to the king for the disposition of divers lands, whereof he had the order and governance; by means whereof, and by his witty demeanour, he grew continually into the king's favour, as ye shall hear after in this history. But first let us resort to the great business about the assurance of all these patents which the king hath given to divers noblemen and other of his servants, wherein Master Cromwell made a continuance of great suit to my lord for the same, that in process of time he served all their turns so that they had their purposes, and he their good wills. Thus rose his name and friendly acceptance with all men. The fame of his honesty and wisdom sounded so in the king's ears that, by reason of his access to the king, he perceived to be in him no less wisdom than fame had made of him report, forasmuch as he had the government and receipts of those lands which I showed you before; and the conference that he had with the king therein enforced the king to repute him a very wise man, and a meet instrument to serve his grace, as it after came to pass.

Sir, now the lords thought long to remove my lord farther from the king, and out of his common trade; wherefore among other of the lords, my Lord of Norfolk said to Master Cromwell, 'Sir,' quoth he, 'me thinketh that the cardinal your master maketh no haste northward; show him, that if he go not away shortly, I will, rather than he should tarry still, tear him with my teeth. Therefore I would advise him to prepare him away as shortly as he can, or else he shall be sent forward.' These words Master Cromwell reported to my lord at his next repair unto him, who then had a just occasion to resort to him for the dispatch of the noblemen's and others' patents...

You have heard herebefore what words the Duke of Norfolk had to Master Cromwell touching my lord's going to the North to his benefice of York, at such time as Master Cromwell declared the same to my lord, to whom my lord answered in this wise: 'Marry, Thomas,' quoth he, 'then it is time to be going, if my Lord of Norfolk take it so. Therefore I pray you go to the king and move his highness in my behalf, and say that I would, with all my heart, go to my benefice at

York, but for want of money; desiring his grace to assist me with some money towards my journey. For ye may say that the last money that I received of his majesty hath been too little to pay my debts, compelled by his counsel so to do; therefore to constrain me to the payment thereof, and his highness having all my goods, hath been too much extremity; wherein I trust his grace will have a charitable respect. Ye may say also to my Lord of Norfolk, and other of the council, that I would depart if I had money.'

'Sir,' quoth Master Cromwell, 'I will do my best.' And after other communication he departed again, and went to London...

Now when Master Cromwell came to the court, he chanced to move my Lord of Norfolk that my lord would gladly depart northward but for lack of money, wherein he desired his assistance to the king. Then went they both jointly to the king, to whom my Lord of Norfolk declared how my lord would gladly depart northward, if he wanted not money to bring him thither; the king thereupon referred the assignment thereof to the council, whereupon they were in divers opinions. Some said he should have none, for he had sufficient of late delivered him; some would he should have sufficient and enough; and some contrariwise would he should have but a small sum; and some thought it much against the council's honour, and much more against the king's high dignity to see him want the maintenance of his estate which the king had given him in this realm; and [who] also hath been in such estimation with the king, and in great authority under him; it should be rather a great slander in foreign realms to the king and his whole council, to see him want that lately had so much, and now so little...

Then after all this they began again to consult in this matter, and after long debating and reasoning about the same, it was concluded, that he should have by the way of prest, a thousand marks out of Winchester Bishoprick, beforehand of his pension, which the king had granted him out of the same, for the king had resumed the whole revenues of the Bishoprick of Winchester into his own hands; yet the king out of the same had granted divers great pensions unto divers noblemen and unto other of his council; so that I do suppose, all things accompted, his part was the least. So that, when this determination was fully concluded, they declared the same to the king, who straightway [commanded] the said thousand marks to be delivered out of hand to Master Cromwell; and so it was. The king, calling Master Cromwell to him secretly, bade him to resort to him again when he had received the said sum of money. And according to the same commandment he repaired again to the king; to whom the king said: 'Show my lord your master, although our council hath not assigned any sufficient sum of money to bear his charges, yet ye shall show him in my behalf, that I will send him a thousand pound, of my benevolence; and tell him that he shall not lack, and bid him be of good cheer.'

Master Cromwell upon his knees most humbly thanked the king on my lord's behalf, for his great benevolence and noble heart towards my lord: 'those comfortable words of your grace,' quoth he, 'shall rejoice him more than three times the value of your noble reward.'

And therewith departed from the king and came to my lord directly to Richmond; to whom he delivered the money, and showed him all the arguments in the council, which ye have heard before, with the progress of the same; and of what money it was, and whereof it was levied, which the council sent him; and of the money which the king sent him, and of his comfortable words; whereof my lord rejoiced not a little, and [was] greatly comforted. And after the receipt of this money my lord consulted with Master Cromwell about his departure, and of his journey, with the order thereof.

19

HARPSFIELD'S LIFE OF MORE (C.1557)

Nicholas Harpsfield (1519–1575) was a historian and a Roman Catholic apologist, who opposed the policies of Henry VIII; he served under Reginald Pole (see Chapter 11). In the reign of Elizabeth I he was imprisoned in the Fleet Prison. His work *The Life and Death of Sir Thomas Moore* [More] was written c.1557. Sir Thomas More (1478–1535), was a lawyer and statesman, and Henry's chancellor, plus Lord High Chancellor from 1529 to 1532. He refused to acknowledge Henry as head of the Church and was executed.

Now upon [More's] resignment of the foresaid office, came Master Thomas Cromwell, then high in the King's favour, to Chelsea to him, with a message from the King. Wherein when they had thoroughly communed together:

'Master Cromwell,' quoth [More], 'you are now entered into the service of a most noble, wise and liberal prince; if you will follow my poor advice, you shall, in your counsel giving to his Grace, ever tell him what he ought to do but never what he is able to do; so shall you show yourself a true, faithful servant and a right worthy Counsellor; for if a lion knew his own strength, hard were it for any man to rule him.'

Which wise and wholesome advice of Sir Thomas More, if the said Cromwell had followed accordingly, he had done the part of a good Counsellor, and perchance preserved the King and the realm from many grievous enormities they fell in, and himself from the utter ruin and destruction he at length fell in.

20

FOXE'S BOOK OF MARTYRS (1563)

John Foxe (1516/17–1587) was an English historian and scholar of religious martyrs, and the author of *Actes and Monuments* (popularly known as *Foxe's Book of Martyrs*), an account of Christian martyrs throughout Western history. His work primarily focuses on the lives and sufferings of Protestants in the 14th and 15th centuries. His account of Cromwell draws heavily on Bandello's (see Chapter 17), and historians regard some of his tales of Cromwell's career as fanciful – although it contains an early account of Cromwell's execution which influenced many other writers. Cromwell's biographer Roger Bigelow Merriman noted: 'nearly every paragraph contains statements which the more trustworthy sources prove to be impossible'.

Thomas Cromwell although born of a simple parentage, and house obscure, through the singular excellency of wisdom, and dexterity of wit wrought in him by God, coupled with like industry of mind, and deserts of life, rose to high preferment and authority; insomuch that by steps and stairs of office and honour, he ascended at length to that, that not only he was made earl of Essex, but also most secret and dear councillor to King Henry, and vicegerent unto his person; which office hath not commonly been supplied, at least not so fruitfully discharged within this realm.

First, as touching his birth, he was born at Putney or thereabouts, being a smith's son, whose mother married afterwards to a shearman [cloth-shearer]. In the simple estate and rude beginnings of this man, as of divers others before him, we may see and learn, that the excellency of noble virtues and heroical prowesses which advance to fame and honour, stand not only upon birth and blood, as privileges only entailed and appropriate to noble houses; but are disposed indifferently, and proceed of the gift of God, who raiseth up the poor abject many times out of the dunghill, and matcheth him in throne with peers and princes.

As touching the order and manner of his coming up, it would be superfluous to discourse what may be said at large; only, by way of story, it may suffice to give a touch of certain particulars, and so to proceed. Although the humble condition and poverty of this man was at the beginning (as it is to many others) a great let and hinderance for virtue to show herself; yet, such was the activity and forward ripeness of nature in him, so pregnant in wit, and so ready he was, in judgment discreet, in tongue eloquent, in service faithful, in stomach courageous, in his pen active, that being conversant in the sight of men, he could not be long unespied, nor yet unprovided of favour and help of friends to set him forward in place and office; neither was any place or office put unto him, whereunto he was not apt and fit. Nothing was so hard which with wit and industry he could not compass: neither was his capacity so good, but his memory was as great in retaining whatsoever he had attained. This well appeared in canning [memorising] the text of the whole New Testament of Erasmus' translation without book, in his journey going and coming from Rome, whereof ye shall hear anon.

Thus, in his growing years, as he shot up in age and ripeness, a great delight came in his mind to stray into foreign countries, to see the world abroad, and to learn experience; whereby he learned such tongues and languages as might better serve for his use hereafter.

And thus, passing over his youth, being at Antwerp he was there retained of the English merchants to be their clerk or secretary, or in some such-like condition placed, pertaining to their affairs.

It happened, the same time, that the town of Boston thought good to send up to Rome, for renewing of their two pardons, one called the greater pardon, the other the lesser pardon. Which thing although it should stand them in great expenses of money (for the pope's merchandise is always dear ware), yet, notwithstanding, such sweetness they had felt thereof, and such gain to come to their town by that Romish merchandise (as all superstition is commonly gainful), that they, like good catholic merchants, and the pope's good customers, thought to spare for no cost, to have their leases again of their pardons renewed, whatsoever they paid for the fine. And yet was all this good religion then, such was the lamentable blindness of that time.

This then being so determined and decreed among my countrymen of Boston, to have their pardons' needs repaired and renewed from Rome, one Geffery Chambers, and another companion, were sent for the messengers, with writings and money no small quantity, well furnished, and with all other things appointed, necessary for so chargeable and costly exploit. Chambers, coming in his journey to Antwerp, and misdoubting himself to be too weak for the compassing of such a weighty piece of work, conferred and persuaded with Thomas Cromwell to associate him in that legacy, and to assist him in the contriving thereof. Cromwell, although perceiving the enterprise to be of no small difficulty, to traverse the pope's court, for the unreasonable expenses amongst those greedy cormorants, yet, having some skill of the Italian tongue, and as yet not grounded in judgment of religion in those his youthful day was at length obtained and content to give the adventure, and so took his journey towards Rome. Cromwell, loth to spend much time, and more loth to spend his money; and again, perceiving that the pope's greedy humour must needs be served with some present or other, (for without rewards there is no doing at Rome,) began to cast with himself, what thing best to devise, wherein he might best serve the pope's devotion.

At length, having knowledge how that the pope's holy tooth

greatly delighted in newfangled strange delicates, and dainty dishes, it came into his mind to prepare certain fine dishes of jelly, after the best fashion, made after our country manner here in England; which, to them of Rome, was not known nor seen before.

This done, Cromwell, observing his time accordingly, as the pope was newly come from hunting into his pavilion, he, with his companions, approached with his English presents, brought in with 'a three man's song' (as we call it) in the English tongue, and all after the English fashion. The pope, suddenly marvelling at the strangeness of the song, and understanding that they were Englishmen, and that they came not empty-handed, willed them to be called in. Cromwell there, showing his obedience, and offering his jolly junkets, 'such as kings and princes only,' said he, 'in the realm of England use to feed upon,' desired the same to be accepted in benevolent part, which he and his companions, as poor suitors unto his Holiness, had there brought and presented, as novelties meet for his recreation, &c.

Pope Julius, seeing the strangeness of the dishes, commanded by and by his cardinal to take the assay [tasting]; who, in tasting thereof, liked it so well, and so likewise the pope after him, that, knowing of them what their suits were, and requiring them to make known the making of that meat, he, incontinent [immediately], without any more ado, stamped both their pardons, as well the greater as the lesser...

These indulgencies, pardons, grants, and relaxations, were given and granted by Pope Nicholas the Fifth, Pope Pius the Second, Pope Sixtus the Fourth, and Pope Julius the Second, of which Pope Julius it seemeth that Cromwell obtained this pardon aforesaid about the year of our Lord 1510: which pardon again afterwards, through the request of King Henry, A.D. 1526, was confirmed by Pope Clement the Seventh. And thus much concerning the pardons of Boston, renewed by means of Thomas Cromwell, of Pope Julius the Second.

All this while it appeareth that Cromwell had yet no sound taste nor judgment of religion, but was wild and youthful, without sense or regard of God and his word, as he himself was wont ofttimes to declare unto Cranmer, archbishop of Canterbury; showing what a ruffian he was in his young days, and how he was in the wars of the duke of Bourbon at the siege of Rome; also what a great doer he was with Geffery Chambers in publishing and setting forth the pardons of Boston every where in churches as he went; and so continued, till, at length, by learning without book the text of the New Testament of Erasmus's translation, in his going and coming from Rome, (as is aforesaid,) he began to be touched, and called to better under-standing.

In this mean time Thomas Wolsey, cardinal of York, began to bear a great port [appearance] in England, and almost to rule all under the king, or rather with the king; so that the freshest wits, and of best towardness, most commonly sought unto him; among whom was also Thomas Cromwell to his service advanced, where he continued a certain space of years, growing up in office and authority, till at length he was preferred to be solicitor [agent/deputy] to the cardinal.

There were also, about the same time, or not much different, in the household of the said cardinal, Thomas More, afterward knight and chancellor of England, and Stephen Gardiner, afterwards bishop of Winchester and of the king's council. All these three were brought up in one household, and all of one standing almost together...

It happened that in this mean season, as Cromwell was placed in this office to be solicitor to the cardinal, the said cardinal had then in hand the building of certain of the colleges, namely, his college in Oxford, called then Frideswide's, now Christ's Church. By reason whereof, certain small monasteries and priors, in divers places of the realm, were, by the said cardinal, suppressed, and the lands seised [granted] to the cardinal's hands; the doing whereof was committed to the charge of Thomas Cromwell: in the expedition whereof he showed himself very forward and industrious, in such sort as in the handling thereof he procured to himself much grudge with divers of the superstitious sort, and with some also of noble calling about the king. And thus was Cromwell first set to work by the cardinal, to suppress religious houses: which was about the year of our Lord 1525.

As this passed on, it was not long but the cardinal, who had gotten up so high, began to come down as fast, first from the chancellorship (in which room was placed Sir Thomas More, as is before said); then he fell into a præmunire [see introductory biography]; so that his household being dissolved, Thomas Cromwell, amongst others, laboured also to be retained into the king's service.

There was at the same time one Sir Christopher Hales, knight, master of the rolls, who, notwithstanding, was then a mighty papist; yet bare he such favour and good liking to Cromwell, that he commended him to the king, as a man most fit for his purpose, having then to do against the pope. But here before is to be understood, that Cromwell had greatly been complained of and defamed, by certain of authority about the king, for his rude manner and homely dealing, in defacing the monks' houses, and in handling of their altars, &c. Wherefore the king, hearing of the name of Cromwell, began to detest the mention of him; neither lacked there some standers-by, who, with reviling words, ceased not to increase and inflame the king's hatred against him: what their names were it shall not need here to recite. Among others, there present at the same hearing, was the Lord Russell, earl of Bedford; whose life Cromwell before had preserved at Bologna, through politic conveyance, at what time the said earl, coming secretly in the king's affairs, was there espied, and therefore being in great danger to be taken, through the means and policy of Cromwell escaped.

This Lord Russell therefore, not forgetting the old benefits past, and with like gratuity willing again to requite what he had received, in a vehement boldness stood forth, to take upon him the defence of Thomas Cromwell, uttering before the king many commendable words in the behalf of him, and declaring withal how, by his singular device and policy, he had done for him at Bologna, being there in the king's affairs in extreme peril. And forasmuch as now his Majesty had to do with the pope, his great enemy, there was (he thought) in all England none so apt for the king's purpose, who could say or do more in that matter, than could Thomas Cromwell: and partly gave the king to understand wherein. The king hearing this, and specially marking the latter end of his talk, was contented and willing to talk with him, to hear and know what he could say.

This was not so privily done, but Cromwell had knowledge, incontinent, that the king would talk with him, and whereupon; and therefore, providing beforehand for the matter, he had in a readiness the copy of the bishops' oath, which they use commonly to make to the pope at their consecration: and so being called for, he was brought to the king in his garden at Westminster; which was about the year of our Lord 1530.

Cromwell, after most loyal obeisance, doing his duty to the king, according as be was demanded, made his declaration in all points; this especially making manifest unto his Highness: how his princely authority was abused within his own realm by the pope and his clergy, who, being sworn unto him, were afterwards dispensed from the same, and sworn anew unto the pope; so that he was but as half a king, and they but half his subjects in his own land: which (said he) was derogatory to his crown, and utterly prejudicial to the common laws of his realm. Declaring, thereupon, how his Majesty might accumulate to himself great riches, as much as all the clergy in his realm were worth, if it so pleased him to take the occasion now offered. The king, giving good ear to this, and liking right well his advice, required if he could avouch that which he spake. All this he could (he said) avouch to be certain so well, as that he had the copy of their own oath to the pope there present to show; and that no less, also, he could manifestly prove, if his Highness would give him leave: and therewith showed the bishops' oath unto the king.

The king, following the vein of his counsel, took his ring off his finger, and first, admitting him into his service, sent him therewith to the convocation-house, among the bishops. Cromwell, coming with the king's signet boldly into the clergy-house, and there placing himself among the bishops, (William Warham being then archbishop,) began to make his oration, declaring unto them the authority of a king, and the office of subjects, and especially the obedience of bishops and churchmen under public laws, necessarily provided for the profit and quiet of the commonwealth. Which laws, notwithstanding, they had all transgressed, and highly offended in derogation of the king's royal estate, falling in the law of præmunire, in that not only they had consented to the power legative of the cardinal; but also, in that they had all sworn to the pope, contrary to the fealty of their sovereign lord the king; and therefore had forfeited to the king all their goods, chattels, lands, possessions, and whatsoever livings they had. The bishops, hearing this, were not a little amazed, and first began to excuse and deny the fact. But after that Cromwell had showed them the very copy of their oath made to the pope at their consecration, and the matter was so plain that they could not deny it, they began to shrink and to fall to entreaty, desiring respite to pause upon the matter. Notwithstanding, the end thereof so fell out, that to be quit of that præmunire by act of parliament, it cost them to the king, for both the provinces, Canterbury and York, no less than one hundred and eighteen thousand eight hundred and forty pounds; which was about the year of our Lord 1530, whereof before you may read more at large.

After this, A.D. 1531, Sir Thomas Cromwell, growing in great favour with the king, was made knight, and master of the king's jewel-house, and shortly after was admitted also into the king's council, which was about the coming in of Queen Anne Bullen [Boleyn]. Furthermore, within three years after the same, A.D. 1534, he was made master of the rolls, Dr. Taylor being discharged.

Thus Cromwell, springing up in favour and honour, after this, in the year 1537, a little before the birth of King Edward, was made knight of the garter, and not long after was advanced to the earldom of Essex, and made great chamberlain of England: over and besides all which honours, he was constituted also vicegerent to the king, representing his person; which office, although it standeth well by the law, yet seldom hath there been seen any besides this Cromwell alone, either to have sustained it, or else to have so furnished the same with counsel and wisdom, as Cromwell did. And thus much hitherto, concerning the steps and degrees of the Lord Cromwell, rising up to dignity and high estate.

Now somewhat would be said, likewise, of the noble acts, the memorable examples, and the worthy virtues, not drowned by ease of honour in him, but increased rather, and quickened by advancement of authority and place, to work more abundantly in the common-wealth: among the which his worthy acts and other manifold virtues, in this one chiefly, above all others, riseth his commendation, for his singular zeal and laborious travail bestowed in restoring the true church of Christ, and subverting the synagogue of antichrist: the abbeys, I mean, and religious houses of friars and monks. For so it pleased Almighty God, by means of the said Lord Cromwell, to induce the king to suppress first the chantries, then the friars' houses and small monasteries, till at length, all the abbeys in England, both great and less, were utterly overthrown and plucked up by the roots. This act and enterprise of his, as it may give a precedent of singular zeal to all realms christened, which no prince yet to this day scarce dare follow; so, to this realm of England, it wrought such benefit and commodity, as the fruit thereof yet remaineth, and will remain still in the realm of England, though we seem little to feel it. Rudely and simply I speak what I suppose, without prejudice of others who can infer any better reason. In the mean time my reason is this, that if God had not raised up this Cromwell as he did, to be the instrument of rooting out these abbeys and cells of strange religion, what other men see I know not for my part, I never yet saw in this realm any such Cromwell since Cromwell's time, whose heart and courage might not sooner have been subverted with the money and bribes of abbots, than he to have subverted any abbey in all England.

Of how great laud and praise this man was worthy, and what courage and stoutness was in him, it may hereby evidently appear unto all men, that he alone, through the singular dexterity of his wit and counsel, brought to pass that which, even unto this day, no prince or king, throughout all Europe, dare or can bring to pass. For whereas Britannia alone, of all other nations, is and hath been, of her own proper nature, most superstitious; this Cromwell, being born of a common or base stock, through a divine method or policy of wit and reason received, suffered, deluded, brake off, and repressed, all the policies, trains [deceptions], malice, and hatred, of friars, monks, religious men, and priests, of which sort there was a great rabble in England. Their houses he subverted throughout all the realm. Afterwards he brought the bishops and archbishops, and the bishop of Winchester himself, although he was the king's chief counsellor, to an order; frustrating and preventing all his enterprises and complaints by a marvellous providence, but, especially, in those things which did tend to the ruin and decay of good men, and such as favoured the gospel; unto whom Cromwell was always as a shield, against the pestiferous enterprises of Winchester.

Briefly, there was continual emulation and mortal dissension between them two, such as Flaccius writeth happened between the wolves and the lambs: for both of them being greatly in the king's favour, the one being much more feared, the other was much better beloved. Either of them excelling in dexterity of wit, howbeit the virtues in the one far exceeded the other; for whereas the bishop of Winchester seemed such a man, to be born for no other purpose but only for the destruction of the good, this man, contrariwise, the Divine Providence had appointed as a remedy to help and preserve many, and to withstand the fury of the bishops; even like as we do see the same ground which bringeth forth most pestiferous poison, the same again also doth bring forth most wholesome and healthful remedies.

It were too long and tedious a declaration here to declare, how many good men, through this man's help and defence, have been relieved and delivered out of danger; of whom a great number after his fall, being deprived of their patron, (as it were,) did shortly after perish: there are many of them, however, yet alive at this present day, who are witnesses of these things which we report, and greater things also than these...

But now, to return to our Christian Camillus, being such a one as if the courts of princes had but a few such counsellors, the Christian commonwealths would, at this day, be in a far better estate. This Cromwell (as I have said) was but of a base stock, but of such virtue as, not without sorrow, we may wish for, even in the most noble families now-a-days. He was first brought up in the cardinal's court, where he did bear several offices, wherein he showed such tokens and likelihood of excellent wit and fidelity, that, in short space, he seemed more meet for the king than for the cardinal...

Now that you have seen what this *malleus monachorum* hath done in defacing the synagogue of the pope, let us see how the same Cromwell again did travail, in setting up Christ's church and congregation.

After that the bishop of Rome's power and authority were banished out of England, the bishops of his sect never ceased to seek all occasion how, either to restore his head again, being broken and wounded, or at least to keep upright those things which yet remained; wherein although their labours were not altogether frustrated, yet had they brought much more to pass, if Cromwell (as a mighty wall and defence of the church) had not resisted continually their enterprises.

It happened that after the abolishing of the pope, certain tumults began to rise about religion; whereupon it seemed good unto King Henry, to appoint an assembly of learned men and bishops, who should soberly and modestly treat and determine those things which pertained unto religion. Briefly, at the king's pleasure, all the learned men, but especially the bishops, assembled, to whom this matter seemed chiefly to belong. Cromwell thought also to be present himself with the bishops, and, by chance, meeting with Alexander Alesius by the way, a Scottish man, brought him with him to the Convocation-house, where all the bishops were assembled together. This was in the year 1537. The bishops and prelates attending upon the coming of Cromwell, as he was come in, rose up and did obeisance unto him as to their vicar-general, and he again saluted every one in their degree, and sat down in the highest place at the table, according to his degree and office; and, after him, every bishop in his order, and doctors. First, over against him, sat the archbishop of Canterbury; then the archbishop of York, the bishops of London, Lincoln, Salisbury, Bath, Ely, Hereford, Chichester, Norwich, Rochester, and Worcester, &c. There Cromwell, in the name of the king, (whose most dear and secret counsellor at that present he was, and lord privy seal, and vicar-general of the realm,) spake these words in manner following:

Right reverend fathers in Christ! The king's Majesty giveth you high thanks that ye have so diligently, without any excuse, assembled hither according to his commandment. And ye be not ignorant that ye be called hither to determine certain controversies, which at this time be moved concerning the Christian religion and faith, not only in this realm, but also in all nations through the world. For the king studieth day and night to set a quietness in the church; and he cannot rest until all such controversies be fully debated and ended, through the determination of you, and of his whole parliament. For, although his special desire is to set a stay for the unlearned people, whose consciences are in doubt what they may believe; and he himself, by his excellent learning, knoweth these controversies well enough, yet he will suffer no common alteration, but by the consent of you and his whole parliament: by which thing ye may perceive both his high wisdom, and also his great love toward you. And he desireth you, for Christ's sake, that all malice, obstinacy, and carnal respect set apart, ye will friendly and lovingly dispute among yourselves of the controversies moved in the church; and that you will conclude all things by the word of God, without all brawling or scolding: neither will his Majesty suffer the Scripture to be wrested and defaced by any glosses, any papistical laws, or by any authority of doctors and councils; and much less will he admit any articles or doctrine not contained in the Scripture, but approved only by continuance of time and old custom, and by unwritten verities, as ye were wont to do. Ye know well enough, that ye be bound to show this service to Christ and to his church; and yet, notwithstanding, his Majesty will give you high thanks, if ye will set and conclude a godly and a perfect unity: whereunto this is the only way and mean, if ye will determine all things by the Scripture, as God commandeth you in Deuteronomy; which thing his Majesty exhorteth and desireth you to do.

When Cromwell had ended this his oration, the bishops rose up altogether, giving thanks unto the king's Majesty, not only for his great zeal toward the church of Christ, but also for his most godly exhortation, worthy so Christian a prince.

Immediately they rose up to disputation, where Stokesley, bishop of London, first of all, being the most earnest champion and maintainer of the Romish decrees, (whom Cromwell a little before had checked by name, for defending unwritten verities,) endeavoured himself, with all his labour and industry, out of the old school glosses, to maintain the seven sacraments of the church: the archbishop of York, and the bishops of Lincoln, Bath, Chichester, and) Norwich, also favoured his part and sect. On the contrary part were the archbishop of Canterbury, the bishops of Salisbury, Ely, Hereford, Worcester, with many others.

After much communication had on either part, and when they had long contended about the testimonies of the doctors, which, as it seemed unto them, dissented and disagreed among themselves, the archbishop of Canterbury at last spake...

When he had ended his oration, Cromwell commanded Alesius, which stood by, (whom he perceived to give attentive ear to that which was spoken,) to show his mind and opinion, declaring to the bishops before, that he was the king's scholar; and therefore desired them to be contented to hear him indifferently...

...The next day, when the bishops were set again, the archbishop of Canterbury, sending his archdeacon, commanded Alesius to abstain from disputation: whereupon he wrote his mind, and delivered it to Cromwell, who afterward showed the same unto the bishops. Thus, through the industry of Cromwell, the colloquies were brought to this end, that albeit religion could not wholly be reformed, yet at that time there was some reformation had throughout all England.

How desirous and studious this good Cromwell was, in the cause of Christ's religion, examples need not to be brought. His whole life was nothing else but a continual care and travail how to advance and further the right knowledge of the gospel, and reform the house of

God: as by so many proclamations above specified, by his means set forth, may well appear, wherein first he caused the people to be instructed in the Lord's Prayer and Creed in English. Then he procured the Scripture also to be read and set forth in the same language, for every Englishman to understand. After that, to rescue the vulgar people from damnable idolatry, he caused certain of the more gross pilgrimages to be destroyed. And further, for the more commodity of the poor sort, who get their living with their daily labour and work of their hands, he provided that divers idle holidays were diminished. Item, he procured for them liberty to eat eggs and white meat in Lent. Furthermore, it was by him also provided, for the better instruction of the people, that beneficed men should be resident in their cures and parishes, there to teach, and to keep hospitality, with many other things else, most fruitfully redressed for the reformation of religion and behoof of Christ's church: as by the proclamations, injunctions, and necessary articles of Christian doctrine above specified, set forth in the king's name, by his means, may more abundantly appear.

Now, to adjoin withal his private benefits, in helping divers good men and women at sundry times out of troubles and great distresses, it would require a long discourse. Briefly, his whole life was full of such examples, being a man to that intent ordained of God (as his deeds well proved) to do many men good, and especially such as were in danger of persecution for religion's sake. Amongst other infinite stories, one or two examples shall suffice for a testimony of his worthy doings; and first, how he helped a poor woman with child, out of great trouble, longing for a piece of meat in time of Lent.

In the year of our Lord 1538, Sir William Forman being mayor of the city of London, three weeks before Easter, the wife of one Thomas Frebarn, dwelling in Paternoster Row, being with child, longed after a morsel of a pig, and told her mind unto a maid dwelling in Abchurch Lane, desiring her, if it were possible, to help her unto a piece. The maid, perceiving her earnest desire, showed unto her husband what his wife had said unto her, telling him that it might chance to cost her her life, and the child's too, which she went withal, if she had it not. Upon this, Thomas Frebarn, her husband, spake to a butter-wife which he knew, that dwelled at Hornsey, named goodwife Fisher, to help him to a pig for his wife, for she was with child, and longed sore to eat of a pig: unto whom the said goodwife Fisher promised, that she would bring him one the Friday following; and so she did, being ready dressed and scalded before. But when she had delivered him the pig, she craftily conveyed one of the pig's feet, and carried it unto Dr. Cox's, at that time being dean of Canterbury, dwelling in Ivy Lane, who, at the time of his dinner, before certain guests which he had bidden, showed this pig's foot, declaring who had the body thereof. And after that they had talked their pleasure, and dinner was done, one of his guests, (being landlord unto Frebarn aforesaid, called Master Garter, and by his office, king at arms,) sent his man unto the said Frebarn, demanding if there were nobody sick in his house: unto whom he answered, that they were all in good health, he gave God thanks. Then said he again, It was told his master, that somebody was sick, or else they would not eat flesh in Lent: unto whom Frebarn made answer, that his wife was with child, and longed for a piece of a pig, and if he could get some for her, he would. Then departed his landlord's man home again.

And, shortly after, his landlord sent for him. But before that he had sent for him, he had sent for the bishop of London's sumner, whose name was Holland, and when this Frebarn was come, he demanded of him if he had not a pig in his house; which he denied not. Then commanded Master Garter the said sumner called Holland, to take him, and go home to his house, and to take the pig, and carry both him, and the pig, unto Dr. Stokesley his master, being then bishop of London: and so he did. Then the bishop, being in his chamber with divers other of the clergy, called this Frebarn before him, and had him in examination for this pig; laying also unto his charge, that he had eaten in his house, that Lent, powdered beef, and calves' heads. Unto whom Frebarn answered, 'My Lord, if the heads were eaten in my house, in whose houses were the bodies eaten? also, if there be either man or woman that can prove, that either I, or any in my house, hath done as your Lordship saith, let me suffer death there-for.'

'You speak,' said he, 'against pilgrimages, and will not take holy bread, or holy water, nor yet go on procession on Palm Sunday; thou art no Christian man.'

'My Lord,' said Frebarn, 'I trust I am a true Christian man, and have done nothing either against God's law or my prince's.'

In the time of this his examination, which was during the space of two hours, divers came unto the bishop; some to have their children confirmed, and some for other causes: unto whom as they came, having the pig before him covered, he would lift up the cloth and show it them, saying, 'How think you of such a fellow as this is? Is not this good meat, I pray you, to be eaten in this blessed time of Lent; yea, and also powdered beef and calves' heads too, besides this!'

After this, the bishop called his sumner [summoner, an ecclesiastical bailiff] unto him, and commanded him to go and carry this Thomas Frebarn, and the pig, openly through the streets into the Old Bailey, unto Sir Roger Cholmley: for the bishop said, he had nothing to do to punish him, for that belonged unto the civil magistrates. And so was Frebarn carried, with the pig before him, to Sir Roger Cholmley's house in the Old Bailey; and he being not at home at that time, Frebarn was brought likewise back again unto the bishop's place with the pig, and there lay in the porter's lodge till it was nine o'clock at night. Then the bishop sent him unto the Compter in the Poultry, by the sumner and other of his servants.

The next day, being Saturday, he was brought before the mayor of London and his brethren, unto Guildhall; but, before his coming, they had the pig delivered unto them by the bishop's officer. Then the mayor and the bench laid unto his charge, (as they were informed from the bishop,) that he had eaten powdered beef and calves' heads in his house the same Lent: but no man was able to come in that would justify it, neither could any thing be found, save only the pig, which (as is before said) was for the preservation of his wife's life, and that she went withal. Notwithstanding the mayor of London said, that the Monday next following he should stand on the pillory in Cheapside, with the one half of the pig on the one shoulder, and the other half on the other.

Then spake the wife of the said Frebarn unto the mayor and the bench, desiring that she might stand there, and not he; for it was the long of her, and not of him. After this they took a satin list [strip of cloth], and tied it fast about the pig's neck, and made Frebarn to carry it, hanging on his shoulder, until he came unto the Compter of the Poultry, from whence he came.

After this was done, the wife of this prisoner took with her an honest woman, the wife of one Michael Lobley, who was well acquainted with divers in the Lord Cromwell's house, unto whom the said woman resorted for some help for this prisoner, desiring them to speak unto their lord and master for his deliverance out of trouble.

It happened that the same time came in Dr. Barnes and Master Barlow, who, understanding the matter by Lobley's wife, went up to the Lord Cromwell, and certified him thereof; who, upon their request, sent for the mayor of the city of London: but what was said unto the lord mayor is unknown, saving that in the afternoon of the same day the wife of the person aforesaid resorted again unto the lord mayor, suing to get her husband delivered out of prison, declaring how that she had two small children, and had nothing to help her and them, but only her husband, who laboured for their livings. Unto whom the mayor answered, 'What come ye to me? You are taken up by the king's council. I supposed, that you had come to desire me that your husband should not stand upon the pillory in Cheapside on Monday next, with the one half of the pig on his one shoulder and the other half on the other.' Also the mayor said unto her, that he could not deliver him, without the consent of the rest of his brethren the aldermen: wherefore he bade her, the next day following, which was the sabbath day, to resort unto Paul's, to St. Dunstan's chapel, and when he had spoken with his brethren, he would then tell her more. Other answer could she not get at that time; wherefore she went unto Master Wilkinson, then being sheriff of London, desiring him to be good unto her, and that she might have her poor husband out of prison.

Unto whom Master Wilkinson answered, 'O woman, Christ hath laid a piece of his cross upon thy neck, to prove whether thou wilt help him to bear it or no:' saying, moreover, unto her, that if the lord mayor had sent him to his Compter, as he sent him to his brother's, he should not of tarried there an hour: and so commanded her to come the next day unto him to dinner, and he would do the best for her he could. So the next day came, and this woman resorted again to Master Wilkinson's according as he bade her, who also had bidden divers guests, unto whom he spake in her behalf. But as they were set at dinner, and she also sitting at the table, when she saw the hot fish come in, she fell down in a swoon, so that for the space of two hours they could keep no life in her. Wherefore they sent her home to her house in Paternoster-row, and then they sent for the midwife, supposing that she would have been delivered incontinent of her child that she went with, (but after that she came somewhat again to herself,) where she lay sick, and kept her bed the space of fifteen weeks after; being not able to help herself, but as she was helped of others, during the time of fifteen weeks.

Now, to show further what became of this pig, whereof we have spoken so much, it was carried into Finsbury field by the bishop of London's sumner, at his master's commandment, and there buried. The Monday following, being the fourth day after that this prisoner aforesaid was apprehended, the mayor of London, with the residue of his brethren, being at Guildhall, sent for the prisoner aforenamed, and demanded sureties of him for his forthcoming, whatsoever here-after should or might be laid unto his charge: but for lack of such sureties as they required, upon his own bond, which was a recogni-sance of twenty pounds, he was delivered out of their hands. But, shortly after he was delivered out of this his trouble, Master Garter, of whom we have spoken before, being his landlord, warned him out of his house, so that in four years after he could not get another, but was constrained to be with other good folks, to his great hinderance and undoing.

Hard it were, and almost out of number, to rehearse the names and stories of all them that felt the gentle help of this good man in some case or other. Where might be remembered the notable deliverance of one Gray, a smith of Bishop's Stortford, who, being accused for denying the sacrament of the altar to be our Saviour, was sent up for the same to London, and there should have been condemned to be burned, but that, by the means of the Lord Cromwell, he was sent home again and delivered. One other example, though it be somewhat long, with the circumstances and all, I will declare: how he helped the secretary that then was to Dr. Cranmer, archbishop of Canterbury, which secretary is yet alive, and can bear present record of the same.

How the Lord Cromwell helped Cranmer's secretary

Mention was made before, how King Henry, in the twenty-first year of his reign, caused the Six Articles to pass, much against the mind, and contrary to the consent, of The archbishop of Canterbury, Thomas Cranmer, who had disputed three days against the same, in the parliament-house, with great reasons and authorities. Which articles, after they were granted and passed by the parliament, the king, for the singular favour which he ever bare to Cranmer, and reverence to his learning, being desirous to know what he had said and objected in the parliament against these articles, or what could be alleged [cited] by learning against the same, required a note of the archbishop of his doings, what he had said and opposed in the parliament touching that matter. And this word was sent to him from the king by Cromwell and other lords of the parliament, whom the king then sent to dine with him at Lambeth, somewhat to comfort again his grieved mind and troubled spirits, as hath been above recited.

Whereupon, when this dinner was finished, the next day after, the archbishop, collecting both his arguments, authorities of Scripture, and doctors together, caused his secretary to write a fair book thereof for the king, after this order. First, the Scriptures were alleged; then the doctors; thirdly, followed the arguments deduced from those authorities. This book was written in his secretary's chamber; where, in a by-chamber, lay the archbishop's almoner. When this book was fair written, and while the secretary was gone to deliver the same unto the archbishop his master, who was (as it then chanced) ridden to Croydon, returning back to his chamber, he found the door shut, and the key carried away to London by the almoner.

At this season also chanced the father of the said secretary to come to the city, by whose occasion it so fell out, that he must needs go to London. The book he could not lay in his chamber, neither durst he commit it to any other person to keep, being straitly charged, in any condition, by the archbishop his master, to be circumspect thereof; so that he determined to go to his father, and to keep the book about him. And so thrusting the book under his girdle, he went over unto Westminster bridge with a sculler, where he entered into a wherry that went to London, wherein were four of the guard, who meant to land at Paul's wharf, and to pass by the king's Highness, who then was in his barge, with a great number of barges and boats about him, then baiting of bears in the water, over against the bank.

These aforesaid yeoman of the guard, when they came against the king's barge, they durst not pass by towards Paul's wharf, lest they should be espied, and therefore entreated the secretary to go with them to the bear baiting, and they would find the means, being of the guard, to make room, and to see all the pastime. The secretary, perceiving no other remedy, assented thereto. When the wherry came nigh the multitude of the boats, they, with poleaxes, got the wherry so far, that being compassed with many other wherries and boats, there was no refuge if the bear should break loose and come upon them; as in very deed, within one Paternoster, the bear brake loose, and came into the boat where the yeoman of the guard were, and the said secretary. The guard forsook the wherry, and went into another barge, one or two of them leaping short, and so fell into the water. The bear and the dogs so shook the wherry wherein the secretary was, that the boat, being full of water, sunk to the ground; and being also, as it chanced, an ebbing tide, he there sat in the end of the wherry up to the middle in water; to whom came the bear and all the dogs. The bear, seeking as it were aid and succour of him, came back with his hinder parts upon him, and so rushing upon him, the book was loosed from his girdle, and fell into the Thames, out of his reach.

The flying of the people after that the bear was loose, from one boat to another, was so cumberous, that divers persons were thrown into the Thames; the king commanding certain men that could swim to strip themselves naked, and to help to save them that were in danger. This pastime so displeased the king, that he bade 'away, away with the bear, and let us all go hence!'

The secretary, perceiving his book to fleet away in the Thames, called to the bearward [keeper of bears] to take up the book. When the bearward had the book in his custody, being an arrant papist, far from the religion of his mistress, (for he was the Lady Elizabeth's bearward, now the queen's Majesty,) ere the secretary could come to land, he had delivered the book to a priest of his own affinity in religion, standing on the bank, who, reading in the book, and perceiving that it was a manifest refutation of the Six Articles, made much ado, and told the bearward, that whosoever claimed the book should surely be hanged. Anon the secretary came to the bearward for his book.

'What,' quoth the bearward, 'dare you challenge this book? Whose servant are you?'

'I am servant to one of the council,' said the secretary, 'and my lord of Canterbury is my master.'

'Yea marry,' quoth the bearward, 'I thought as much: you be like, I trust,' quoth the bearward, 'to be both hanged for this book.'

'Well,' said he, 'it is not so evil as you take it, and, I warrant you, my Lord will avouch the book to the king's Majesty. But I pray you let me have my book, and I will give you a crown to drink.'

'If you will give me five hundred crowns, you shall not have it,' quoth the bearward.

With that the secretary departed from him, and understanding the malicious frowardness of the bearward, he learned that Blage, the grocer in Cheapside, might do much with the bearward, to whom the secretary brake this matter, requiring him to send for the bearward to supper, and he would pay for the whole charge therin; and besides that, rather than he would forego his book after this sort, the bear-ward should have twenty shillings to drink. The supper was prepared; the bearward was sent for and came. After supper the matter was treated of, and twenty shillings offered for the book. But do what could be done, neither friendship, acquaintance, nor yet reward of money, could obtain the book out of his hands, but that the same should be delivered unto some of the council that would not so slightly look on so weighty a matter, as to have it redeemed for a supper, or a piece of money. The honest man, Master Blage, with many good reasons, would have persuaded him not to be stiff in his own conceit, declaring that in the end he should nothing at all prevail of his purpose, but be laughed to scorn; getting neither penny nor praise for his travail. He, hearing that, rushed suddenly out of the doors from his friend Master Blage, without any manner of thanks-giving for his supper, more like a bearward, than like an honest man. When the secretary saw the matter so extremely to be used against him, be then thought it expedient to fall from any further practising of entreaty with the bearward, as with him that seemed rather to be a bear himself, than the master of the beast; determining the next morning to make the Lord Cromwell privy of the chance that happened.

So, on the next day, as the Lord Cromwell went to the court, the secretary declared the whole matter unto him, and how he had offered him twenty shillings for the finding thereof. 'Where is the fellow?' quoth the Lord Cromwell.

'I suppose,' said the secretary, 'that he is now in the court, attending to deliver the book unto some of the council'

'Well,' said the Lord Cromwell, 'it maketh no matter; go with me thither, and I shall get you your book again.'

When the Lord Cromwell came into the hall of the court, there stood the bearward, with the book in his hand, waiting to have deliv-ered the same unto Sir Anthony Brown, or unto the bishop of Winchester, as it was reported. To whom the Lord Cromwell said, 'Come hither, fellow! what book hast thou there in thy hand?' and with that snatched the book out of his hand, and looking in the book, he said, 'I know this hand well enough. This is your hand,' said he to the secretary. 'But where hadst thou this book?' quoth the Lord Cromwell to the bearward.

'This gentleman lost it two days ago in the Thames,' said the bearward.

'Dost thou know whose servant he is?' said the Lord Cromwell.

'He saith,' quoth the bearward, 'that he is my Lord of Canterbury's servant.'

'Why then didst thou not deliver to him the book, when he required it?' said the Lord Cromwell. 'Who made thee so bold, as to detain and withhold any book or writing from a councillor's servant, especially being his secretary? It is more meet for thee to meddle with thy bears, than with such writing; and were it not for thy mistress' sake, I would set thee fast by the feet, to teach such malapert knaves to meddle with councillors' matters. Had not money been well bestowed upon such a good fellow as this is? that knoweth not a councillor's man from a cobbler's man!'

And with those words the Lord Cromwell went up into the king's chamber of presence, and the archbishop's secretary with him, where he found, in the chamber, the lord of Canterbury. To whom he said, 'My lord! I have found here good stuff for you, (showing to him the paper book that he had in his hand,) ready to bring both you, and this good fellow your man, to the halter; namely, if the knave bearward, now in the hall, might have well compassed it.'

At these words the archbishop smiled, and said, 'He that lost the book is like to have the worst bargain, for besides that he was well washed in the Thames, he must write the book fair again:' and, at these words, the Lord Cromwell cast the book unto the secretary, saying, 'I pray thee, Morice! go in hand therewith, by-and-by, with all expedition, for it must serve a turn.'

'surely, my Lord, it somewhat rejoiceth me,' quoth the Lord Cromwell, 'that the varlet might have had of your man twenty shillings for the book, and now I have discharged the matter with never a penny, and shaken him well up for his over-much malapert-ness. I know the fellow well enough,' quoth he, 'there is not a ranker papist within this realm than he is, most unworthy to be a servant unto so noble a princess.'

And so, after humble thanks given to the Lord Cromwell, the said Morice departed with his book, which, when he again had fair written it, was delivered to the king's Majesty by the said Lord Cromwell, within four days after.

The Lord Cromwell not forgetting his old friends and benefactors.

It is commonly seen, that men advanced once from base degree to ample dignities, do rise also, with fortune, into such insolency and exaltation of mind, that not only they forget themselves, what they were, and from whence they came, but also cast out of remembrance all their old friends and former acquaintance, which have been to them before beneficial. From which sort of men how far the courteous condition of this Christian earl did differ, by divers examples it may appear; as by a certain poor woman keeping some time a victualling-house about Hounslow, to whom the said Lord Cromwell remained in debt for certain old reckonings, to the sum of forty shillings. It happened that the Lord Cromwell, with Cranmer archbishop of Canterbury, riding through Cheapside towards the court, in turning his eye over the way, and there espying this poor woman, brought now in need and misery, eftsoons caused her to be called unto him; who, being come, after certain questions, asked of her (if she were not such a woman, and dwelling in such a place); at last, he demanded if he were not behind for a certain payment of money between him and her. To whom, with reverent obeisance, she confessed that he owed her money for a certain old reckoning, which was yet unpaid; whereof she stood now in great necessity, but never durst call upon him, nor could come at him, to require her right. Then the Lord Cromwell, sending the poor woman home to his house, and one of his servants withal, that the porter should let her in, after his return from the court not only discharged the debt which he owed, but also gave her a yearly pension of four pounds, and a livery every year while she lived.

The like courtesy the said Lord Cromwell showed also to a certain Italian, who, in the city of Florence, had showed him much kindness in succouring and relieving his necessity, as in this story following may appear; which story, set forth and compiled in the Italian tongue by Bandello [see Chapter 17], and imprinted at Lucca, by Busdrago, A. D. 1554, I thought here to insert, with the whole order and circumstance thereof, as it is reported.

'Not many years past,' saith the author, 'there was in Florence a merchant, whose name was Francis, descended from the noble and ancient family of the Frescobalds. This gentleman was naturally endued with a noble and liberal mind, unto whom, also, through prosperous success and fortunate luck in his affairs and doings, much abundance of riches increased, so that he grew in great wealth, having his coffers replenished with many heaps of much treasure. According to the custom of merchants, he used his trade into many countries, but chiefly into England, where long time he lived, sojourning in London, keeping house to his great commendation and praise.

'It happened that Francis Frescobald, being in Florence, there appeared before him a poor young man, asking his alms for God's sake. Frescobald, as he earnestly beheld this ragged stripling, who was not so disguised in his tattered attire, but that his countenance gave signification of much towardness and virtue in him, with conformity of manners agreeing to the same, being moved with pity, demanded of what country he was, and where he was born. 'I am, sir,' quoth he, 'of England, and my name is Thomas Cromwell. My father is a poor man, and by his occupation a cloth-shearer. I am strayed from my country, and am now come into Italy, with the camp of Frenchmen that were overthrown at Garigliano, where I was the page to a footman, carrying after him his pike and burganet.' Frescobald, partly considering the present state of this young man, and partly for the love he bare to the English nation, of whom he had received, in times past, sundry pleasures, received him into his house, and with such courtesy entertained his guest, that at his departure, when he was in mind to return to his country, he provided such necessaries as he in any way needed. He gave him both horse and new apparel, and sixteen ducats of gold in his purse, to bring him into his country. Cromwell, rendering his hearty thanks, took leave of his host, and returned into England. This Cromwell was a man of noble courage, and heroical spirit, given to enterprise great matters, very liberal, and a grave councillor, &c. But to our purpose. At what time Cromwell was so highly favoured of his prince, and advanced to such dignity as is aforesaid, Francis Frescobald (as it many times happeneth to merchants) was, by many misfortunes and great losses, cast back, and become very poor. For, according to conscience and equity, he paid whatsoever was due to any others from himself; but such debts as were owing unto him, he could by no means obtain: yet, calling further to remembrance that in England, by certain merchants, there was due to him the sum of fifteen thousand ducats, he so purposed with himself, that if he could recover that money, he would well content himself, and no longer deal in his trade of merchants, but quietly pass over the rest of his days.

'All things prepared for his journey, he, setting forward towards England, at last arrived at London, having utterly forgotten what courtesy long before he had showed to Cromwell; which is the property always of a good nature, for a man to forget what benefits he hath showed to others, but to keep in mind continually what he hath received of others. Frescobald, thus being now arrived at London, and there travelling earnestly about his business, it chanced him, by the way, to meet with this nobleman, as he was riding towards the court; whom, as soon as the said Lord Cromwell had espied, and had earnestly beheld, he bethought with himself that he should be the man of Florence, at whose hands, in times past, he had received so gentle entertainment: and thereupon suddenly alighting, (to the great admiration of those that were with him,) in his arms he gently embraced the stranger, and with a broken voice, scarce able to refrain tears, he demanded if he were not Francis Frescobald the Florentine. 'Yea, sir,' he answered, 'and your humble servant.' 'My servant?' quoth Cromwell. 'No, as you have not been my servant in times past, so will I not now account you otherwise than my great and especial friend; assuring you that I have just reason to be sorry, That you, knowing what I am, (or, at least, what I should be,) will not let me understand of your arriving in this land; which, known unto me, truly I should have paid part of that debt, which I confess to owe you: but, thanked be God! I have yet time. Well, sir, in conclusion, you are heartily welcome: but, having now weighty affairs in my princes cause, you must hold me excused, that I can no longer tarry with you. Therefore, at this time I take my leave, desiring you, with the faithful mind of a friend, that you forget not this day to come to my house to dinner.' And then, remounting his horse, he passed to the court.

'Frescobald, greatly marvelling with himself who this lord should be, at last, after some pause his remembrance better called home, he knew him to be the same, whom long before (as you have heard) he had relieved in Florence; and thereat he not a little joyed, especially considering how that, by his means, he should the better recover his due.

'The hour of dinner drawing near, he repaired to the house of this honourable councillor, where, walking a while in his base court, he attended his coming. The lord shortly returned from the court, and no sooner dismounted, but he again embraced this gentleman with so friendly a countenance, that both the lord admiral, and all the other noblemen of the court, being then in his company, did not a little marvel thereat. Which thing when the Lord Cromwell perceived, he said, turning towards them, and holding Frescobald fast by the band, 'Do ye not marvel, my Lords,' quoth he, 'that I seem so glad of this man? This is he by whose means I have achieved the degree of this my present calling: and because ye shall not be ignorant of his courtesy when I greatly needed, I shall tell it you.' And so there declared he unto them every thing in order, according as before hath been recited unto you. His tale finished, holding him still by the hand, he entered his house; and coming into the chamber where his dinner was prepared, he sat him down to the table, placing his best-welcomed guest next unto him.

The dinner ended, and the lords departed, he would know what occasion had brought Frescobald to London. Francis, in few words, opened his cause, truly telling, that from great wealth he was fallen into poverty, and that his only portion to maintain the rest of his life, was fifteen thousand ducats which were owing him in England, and two thousand in Spain. Whereunto the Lord Cromwell, answering again, said, Touching the things, Master Frescobald! that be already past, although it cannot now be undone by man's power, nor by policy called again, which hath happened unto you by the unstable condition and mutability of this world, altering to and fro; yet is not your sorrow so peculiar to yourself alone, but that, by the bond of mutual love, I must also bewail with you this your state and condition: which state and condition of yours, though it may work in you matter of just heaviness, yet, notwithstanding, to the intent you may receive, in this your heavy distress, some consolation for your old courtesy, showed to me in times past, the like courtesy now requireth of me again, that I, likewise, should repay some portion of that debt wherein I stand bound unto you; according as the part of a thankful man bindeth me to do, in requiting your benefits on my part heretofore received. And this further I avouch on the word of a true friend, that during this life and state of mine, I will never fail to do for you, wherein my authority may prevail to supply your lack and necessity: and so let these few words suffice to give you knowledge of my friendly meaning. But let me delay the time no longer.

Then, taking him by the hand, he led him into his chamber, whence, after that every man by his commandment was departed, he locked fast the door. Then, opening a coffer full heaped with treasure, he first took out sixteen ducats, and, delivering them to Frescobald, he said; Lo here, my friend! is your money which you lent me at my departure from Florence, and here are other ten which you bestowed on my apparel, with ten more that you disbursed for the horse I rode away on. But, considering you are a merchant, it seemeth to me not honest to return your money without some consideration for the long detaining of it. Take you, therefore, these four bags, and in every one of them are four hundred ducats: these you shall receive and enjoy from the hands of your assured friend.'

'Frescobald, although from great wealth he was brought to a low ebb, and almost an utter decay, yet, expressing the virtue of a modest mind, after gentle thanks given to the Lord Cromwell for his exceeding kindness showed, courteously would have refused that which was offered, had not the other enforced him against his will to receive it. This done, he caused Frescobald to give him a note of the names of all his debtors, and the sum that from every one of them was owing him. This schedule he delivered to one of his servants, unto whom he gave charge diligently to search out such men whose names were therein contained, if they were within any part of the. realm; and then straitly to charge them to make payment of those sums within fifteen days, or else to abide the hazard of his displeasure. The servant so well performed his master's commandment, that in very short time they made payment of the whole sum; and if it had liked Frescobald so to have demanded, they should have answered to the uttermost, such commodity as the use of his money in so many years would have given him profit: but he, contented with his principal, would demand no further; by which means he got both hearty love and great estimation, and the more, for that he was so dear to the Lord Cromwell, and so highly esteemed of him.

And during all this time, Frescobald continually lodged in the house of the Lord Cromwell, who ever gave him such entertainment as he had right well deserved, and oftentimes moved him to abide here in England, offering him the loan of threescore thousand ducats for the space of four years, if he would continue, and make his bank in London. But Frescobald, who desiredto return into his country, and there quietly to continue the rest of his life, with the great favour of the Lord Cromwell, after many thanks for his high and noble entertainment, departed towards his desired home, where, richly arriving, he gave himself quietly to live. But this wealth he small time enjoyed, for in the first year of his return he died.'

So plentiful was the life of this man in such fruits, full of singular gratitude and courtesy, that to rehearse all it would require too long a tractation. Yet one example amongst many others I may not overpass, whereby we may evidently consider, or rather marvel at, the lowly mind of such a person in so high a state and place of honour. For as he, coming with others of the lords of the council and commissioners, to the house of Shene, about the examination of certain monks, which there denied the king's supremacy, after the examination done was there sitting at dinner, it chanced him to spy afar off a certain poor man, who there served to sweep their cells and cloisters, and to ring the bells: whom when the Lord Cromwell had well advised, he sent for the poor man to come unto him, and, before all the table, most lovingly and friendly called him by his name, took him by the hand, and asked how he did, with many other good words; and turning therewith to the lords, 'My lords!' quoth he, 'see you this poor man? This man's father hath been a great friend to me in my necessity, and hath given me many a meal's meat.' Then said he unto the poor man, 'Come unto me, and I will provide for thee, and thou shalt not lack so long as I live.' Such as were there present, and saw and heard the same, being alive at the second edition hereof, report it to be true.

In this worthy and noble person, besides divers other eminent virtues, three things especially are to be considered, to wit, flourishing authority, excelling wisdom, and fervent zeal to Christ and to his gospel. First, as touching his fervent zeal in setting forward the sincerity of Christian faith, sufficient is to be seen before by the injunctions, proclamations, and articles above specified, that more cannot almost be wished in a nobleman, and scarce the like hath been seen in any.

Secondly, with his wisdom and policy no less singular, joined with his Christian zeal, he brought great things to pass, as well on this side the sea, as in the other parts beyond. But especially his working was to nourish peace abroad with foreign realms, as may be well, by the king's letters and instructions, sent by this means to his ambassadors resident both with the emperor, the French king, and the king of Scots, and also with the pope, may well appear; in all whose courts, such watch and espial he had, that nothing there was done, nor pretended, whereof he before had not intelligence. Neither was there any spark of mischief kindling ever so little against the king and the realm, which he, by wit and policy, did not quench and keep down; and where policy would not serve to obtain peace, yet by money he bought it out; so that during all the time of Cromwell's prosperity, the king never had war with any foreign nation: notwithstanding, tha both the pope, the emperor, and the kings of France and Scotland, were mightily bent and incensed against him.

Thus, as the prudent policy of this man was ever circumspect abroad, to stay the realm from foreign wars; so his authority was no less occupied in keeping good order and rule at home: first, in hampering the popish prelates, and disappointing their subtle devices; secondly, in bridling and keeping other unruly subjects under subjection and discipline of the laws; whereby as he was a succour and refuge to all godly persons, so was he a terror to the evil-doers; so that not the presence of him only, but also the hearing of the coming of Cromwell, brake many frays, and much evil rule, as well appeared by a certain notorious fray or riot, appointed to be fought by a company of ruffians in the street of London called Paternoster Row; where carts were set on both sides, prepared on purpose to enclose them, that none might break in to part them. It happened that as this desperate skirmish should begin, the Lord Cromwell, coming the same time from the court through Paul's Church-yard, and entering into Cheap, had intelligence of the great fray toward, and because of the carts he could not come at them, but was forced to go about the Little Conduit, and so came upon them through Pannier Alley. Thus, as the conflict began to wax hot, and the people were standing by in great expectation to see them fight, suddenly, at the noise of the Lord Cromwell's coming, the camp brake up, and the ruffians fled, neither could the carts keep in those so courageous campers, but well was he that first could be gone. And so ceased this tumultuous outrage, without any other parting; only through the authority of the Lord Cromwell's name.

One example more of the like affinity cometh here in mind, which ought not to be omitted, concerning a certain servingman of the like ruffianly order; who, thinking to dissever himself from the common usage of all other men in strange newfangleness of fashions by himself, (as many there be whom nothing doth please which is daily seen and received,) used to go with his hair hanging about his ears down unto his shoulders, after a strange monstrous manner,. (counterfeiting belike the wild Irishmen, or else Crimisus, the Trojan, whom Virgil speaketh of,) as one weary of his own English fashion; or else as one who, ashamed to be seen like a man, would rather go like a woman; or like to one of the Gorgon sisters; but most of all like to himself; that is, like to a ruffian, that could not tell how to go.

As this ruffian, ruffling thus with his locks, was walking in the streets, as chance was, who should meet him but the Lord Cromwell! who, beholding the deform and unseemly manner of his disguised going, full of much vanity and hurtful example, called the man, to question with him whose servant he was: which being declared, then was it demanded whether his master or any of his fellows so to go with such hair about their shoulders as he did, or no: which when he denied, and was not able to yield any reason for refuge of that his monstrous diguising, at length he fell to this excuse, that he had made a vow. To this the Lord Cromwell answered again, that forasmuch as he had made himself a votary, he would not force him to break his vow, but until his vow should be expired, he should lie the mean time in prison: and so sent him immediately to the Marshalsea, where he endured; till at length this Intonsus Cato, being persuaded by his master to cut his hair, by suit and petition of friends, he was brought again to the Lord Cromwell, with his head polled according to the accustomed sort of his other fellows; and so was dismissed.

Hereunto also pertaineth the example of Friar Bartley, who, wearing still his friar's cowl after the suppression of religious houses,

Cromwell, coming through Paul's Church-yard, and espying him in Rheines's shop, 'Yea,' said he, 'will not that cowl of yours he left off yet? And if I hear, by one o'clock, that this apparel be not changed, thou shalt be hanged immediately, for example to all others.' And so, putting his cowl away, he durst never wear it after...

Long it were to recite what innumerable fits this worthy councillor, by his prudent policy, his grave authority, and perfect zeal, wrought and brought to pass in the public realm, and especially in the church of England; what good orders he established, what wickedness and vices he suppressed, what corruptions he reformed, what abuses he brought to light; what crafty jugglings, what idolatrous deceptions, and superstitious illusions, he detected and abolished out of the church. What posterity will ever think the church of the pope, pretending such religion, to have been so wicked, so long to abuse the people's eyes with an old rotten stock, called the Rood of Grace, wherein a man should stand enclosed, with a hundred wires within the rood, to make the image goggle with the eyes, to nod with his head, to hang the lip, to move and shake his jaws, according as the value was of the gift which was offered? If it were a small piece of silver, the image would hang a frowning lip; if it were a piece of gold, then should his jaws go merrily. Thus miserably were the people of Christ abused, their souls seduced, their senses beguiled, and their purses spoiled, till this idolatrous forgery, at last, by Cromwell's means, was disclosed, and the image, with all his engines, showed openly at Paul's Cross, and there torn in pieces by the people. The like was done by the blood of Hayles, which, in like manner, by Cromwell was brought to Paul's Cross, and there proved to be the blood of a duck. Who would have judged, but that the maid of Kent had been a holy woman, and a prophetess inspired, had not Cromwell and Cranmer tried her at Paul's Cross, to be a strong and lewd impostor. What should I speak of Darvel Gartheren, of the rood of Chester, of Thomas Becket, of our Lady of Walsingham, with an infinite multitude more of the like affinity? all which stocks and blocks of cursed idolatry, Cromwell, stirred up by the providence of God, removed them out of the people's way, that they might walk more safely in the sincere service of Almighty God.

While the Lord Cromwell was thus blessedly occupied in profiting the commonwealth, and in purging the church of Christ, it happened to him, as commonly it doth to all good men, that where any excellency of virtue appeareth, there envy creepeth in; and where true piety seeketh most after Christ, there some persecution followeth withal.

Thus, I say, as he was labouring in the commonwealth, and doing good to the poor afflicted saints, helping them out of trouble, the malice of his enemies so wrought, continually hung for matter against him, that they never ceased, till in the end, false trains and crafty surmises, they brought him out of the king's favour.

The chief and principal enemy against him was Stephen Gardiner, bishop of Winchester, who, ever disdaining and envying the state and felicity of the Lord Cromwell, and now taking his occasion by the marriage of Lady Anne of Cleves, being a stranger and foreigner, put in the king's ears what a perfect thing it were for the quiet of the realm, and establishment of the king's succession, to have an English queen, and prince that were mere English; so that, in conclusion, the king's affection, the more it was diminished from the late married Anne of Cleves, the less favour he bare unto Cromwell. Besides this Gardiner, there lacked not other back friends also, and ill-willers in the court about the king, which little made for Cromwell, both for his religion which they maligned, and for other private grudges also, incident by the way.

Over and beside which, it is, moreover, supposed, that some part of displeasure might arise against him by reason of a certain talk which happened a little before at Lambeth; at what time the king, after the making of. the Six Articles, sent the said Lord Cromwell his vicegerent, with the two dukes of Norfolk and Suffolk, with all the lords of the parliament, to Lambeth, to dine with the archbishop, (who mightily had disputed and alleged in the parliament against the said articles,) to cheer and comfort his daunted spirits again.

There the said Cromwell, with the other noble lords, sitting with the archbishop at his table in talk, as every lord brought forth his sentence in commendation of Cranmer, to signify what good will both the king and they bare unto him; among the rest, one of the company, entering into a comparison between the said Thomas Cranmer and Thomas Wolsey, late cardinal of York, declared that Cranmer, in his judgment, was much to be preferred for his mild and gentle nature, whereas the cardinal was a stubborn and a churlish prelate, and one that could never abide any noble man. 'And that,' said he 'know you well enough, my Lord Cromwell! for he was your master,' &c.: At these words the Lord Cromwell, being somewhat touched to hear the cardinal's service so cast in his teeth, inferred again, saying, that he could not deny but he was servant some time to Cardinal Wolsey, neither did repent the same; for he received of him both fee, meat, and drink, and other commodities: but yet he was never so far in love with him, as to have waited upon him to Rome, if he had been chosen pope, as he understood that he would have done, if the case had so fallen out. Which when the other had denied to be true, Cromwell still persisted, affirming the same, and showing, moreover, what number of florins he should have received, to be his admiral, and to have safely conducted him to Rome, in case he had been elected bishop of Rome. The party, not a little moved with these words, told him, he lied. The other again affirmed it to be true. Upon this, great and high words rose between them; which contention, although it was, through entreaty of the archbishop and other nobles, somewhat pacified for the time, yet it might be, that some fitter root of grudge remained behind, which afterwards grew unto him to some displeasure. And this was A. D. 1539, in the month of July.

After this, the next year following, which was 1540, in the month of April, was holden a parliament; which, after divers prorogations, was continued till the month of July. On the tenth of June in the said year, the Lord Cromwell, being in the council-chamber, was suddenly apprehended, and committed to the Tower of London: whereat as many good men, who knew nothing but truth by him, did lament and prayed heartily for him, so more there were, on the contrary side, that rejoiced, especially of the religious sort, and of the clergy, such as had been in some dignity before in the church, and now, by his means, were put from it. For indeed such was his nature, that in all his doings he could not abide any kind of popery, or of false religion creeping under hypocrisy; and less could he abide the ambitious pride of popish prelacy, which, professing all humility, was so elated in pride, that kings could not rule in their own realms for them. These snuffing prelates as he could never abide, so they again hated him as much, which was the cause of shortening his days, and of bringing him to his end; so that on the seventeenth day of the month aforesaid, he was attainted by parliament.

In that attainder, divers and sundry crimes, surmises, objections, and accusations, were brought against him: but chiefly, and above all others, he was charged and accused of heresy, for that he was a supporter of them whom they recounted for heretics; as Barnes, Clark, and many others, whom, by his authority, and letters written to sheriffs and justices in divers shires, he had rescued, and discharged out prison. Also that he did divulgate and disperse abroad among the king's subjects great numbers of books, containing (as they said) manifest matter of much heresy, diffidence, and misbelief. Item, that he caused to be translated into our English tongue, books comprising matter expressly against the sacrament of the altar; and that after the translation thereof, he commended and maintained the same for good and Christian doctrine. Over and besides all this, they brought in certain witnesses, (what they were, the attainder expresseth not,) which most especially pressed (or rather oppressed) him with heinous words spoken against the king in the church of St. Peter the Poor, in the month of March, in the thirtieth year of the king's reign; which words if they be true, as the attainder doth purport, three things I have here much to marvel at. First, if his adversaries had so sure hold and matter against him, then what should move them to make such hasty speed, in all post haste to have him despatched and rid out of the way, and in no case could abide him to come to his purgation? which if he might have done, it is not otherwise to bethought, but he would easily have cleared himself thereof.

Secondly, this I marvel, that if the words had been so heinous against the king as his enemies did pretend, why then did those witnesses who heard those words in St. Peter's church in the thirtieth year of the king's reign, conceal the said words of such treason so long, the space almost of two years, and now uttered the same in the two-and-thirtieth year of the king's reign, in the month of July.

Thirdly, here is again to be marvelled, if the king had known or believed these words to be true, and that Cromwell had been indeed such a traitor to his person, why then did the king, so shortly after, lament his death, wishing to have his Cromwell alive again? What prince will wish the life of him whom he suspecteth undoubtedly to be a traitor to his life and person? Whereby it may appear what judgment the king had of Cromwell in himself, howsoever the parliament, by sinister information, was otherwise incensed to judge upon him.

Such malicious makebates about princes and parliaments never lacked in commonweals...

In the mean season, howsoever the cause of the Lord Cromwell standeth true or false, this is certain, that Stephen Gardiner lacked not a head, nor yet assisters, which cunningly could fetch this matter about, and watch their time, when the king, being disposed to marry another wife, which was the Lady Katharine Howard, immediately after the beheading of the Lord Cromwell, did repudiate Lady Anne of Cleves, which otherwise it is to be thought, during the life of Cromwell could not so well be brought to pass.

But these things being now done and past, let us pass them over, and return again from whence we digressed, that is, to the Lord Cromwell, being now attainted and committed to the Tower; who, so long as he went with full sail of fortune, how moderately and how temperately he did ever bear himself in his estate, before hath been declared. So now the said Lord Cromwell, always one man, by the contrary wind of adversity being overblown, received the same with no less constancy and patience of a Christian heart; neither yet was he so unprovided of counsel and forecast, but that he did foresee this tempest long before it fell, and also prepared for the same; for two years before, smelling the conspiracy of his adversaries, and fearing what might happen, he called unto him his servants, and there, showing unto them in what a slippery state he stood, and also perceiving some stormy weather already to gather, required them to look diligently to their order and doings, lest, through their default, any occasion might rise against him. And furthermore, before the time of his apprehension, such order he took for his servants, that many of them, especially the younger brethren, which had little else to take unto, had honestly left for them in their friends' hands to relieve them; whatsoever should him befall.

Briefly, such a loving and kind master he was to his servants, that be provided aforehand almost for them all; insomuch, that he gave to twelve children, which were his musicians, twenty pounds a piece, and so committed them to their friends, of whom some yet remain alive, who both enjoyed the same, and also gave record of this to be true.

Furthermore, being in the Tower a prisoner, how quietly he bare it, how valiantly he behaved himself, how gravely and discreetly be answered and entertained the commissioners sent unto him, it is worthy noting. Whatsoever articles and interregatories they propounded, they could put nothing unto him, either concerning matters ecclesiastical or temporal, wherein he was not more ripened, and more furnished in every condition, than they themselves.

Amongst the rest of those commissioners who came unto him, one there was, whom the Lord Cromwell desired to carry for him a letter to the king; which when he refused, saying that he would carry no letter to the king from a traitor, then the Lord Cromwell desired him at least to do from him a message to the king. To that the other was contented, and granted, so that it were not against his allegiance. Then the Lord Cromwell, taking witness of the other lords, what he had promised, 'You shall commend me,' said he, 'to the king, and tell him, by that he hath so well tried and throughly proved you as I have done, he shall find you as false a man as ever came about him.'

Besides this, he wrote also a letter from the Tower to the king, whereof when none durst take the carriage upon him, Sir Ralph Sadler (whom he also had preferred to the king before, being ever trusty and faithful unto him) went unto the king to understand his pleasure, whether he would permit him to bring the letter or not; which when the king had granted, the said Master Sadler, as he was required, presented the letter unto the king, which he commanded thrice to be read unto him, insomuch that the king seemed to be moved therewith.

At last, three years after all this was done, Cromwell being circum-vented with the malicious craft and policy of divers, that, by occasion of mention made touching the king's divorce with the Lady Anne of Cleves, he had said these words, 'That he wished his dagger in him that had dissolved or broken that marriage;' hereupon it was objected against him by Thomas, duke of Norfolk, and others, that it was spoken against the king, who, at that time being in love with Katharine Howard, was the chief cause and author of that divorce. Whereupon divers of the nobles conspiring against him, some for hatred, and some for religion's sake, he was cast into the Tower of London; where, as it happened, (as it were by a certain fatal destiny,) that whereas he, a little before, had made a law, that whosoever was cast into the Tower, should be put to death without examination, he himself suffered by the same law. It is said, (which also I do easily credit,) that he made this violent law, not so much for any cruelty or tyranny, as only for a certain secret purpose, to have entangled the bishop of Winchester, who, albeit he was, without doubt, the most violent adversary of Christ and his religion, notwithstanding, God, peradventure, would not have his religion set forth by any wicked cruelty, or otherwise than was meet and convenient.

Notwithstanding, by reason of the act of parliament before passed, the worthy and noble Lord Cromwell, oppressed by his enemies, and condemned in the Tower, and not coming to his answer, on the twenty-eighth day of July, A. D. 1540, was brought to the scaf-fold on Tower-bill, where he said these words following [see Cromwell's actual letter in Chapter 12]:

> I am come hither to die, and not to purge myself, as some think, peradventure, that I will: for if I should so do, I were a very wretch and a miser. I am, by the law, condemned to die, and thank my Lord

God that hath appointed me this death for mine offence. For since the time that I have had years of discretion, I have lived a sinner, and offended my Lord God; for the which I ask him heartily forgiveness. And it is not unknown to many of you, that I have been a great travailler in this world, and being but of a base degree, was called to high estate; and since the time I came thereunto I have offended my prince, for the which I ask him heartily forgiveness, and beseech you all to pray to God with me, that He will forgive me. O Father, forgive me! O Son, forgive me! O Holy Ghost, forgive me! O three persons in one God, forgive me! And now I pray you that be here, to bear me record, I die in the catholic faith, not doubting in any article of my faith, no, nor doubting in any sacrament of the church. Many have slandered me, and reported that I have been a bearer of such as have maintained evil opinions; which is untrue: but I confess, that like as God, by his Holy Spirit, doth instruct us in the truth, so the devil is ready to seduce us; and I have been seduced. But bear me witness, that I die in the catholic faith of the holy church. And I heartily desire you to pray for the king's Grace, that he may long live with you in health and prosperity; and that after him, his son, Prince Edward, that goodly imp, may long reign over you. And once again I desire you to pray for me, that so long as life remaineth in this flesh, I waver nothing in my faith.

And so making his prayer, which was long, but not so long as both godly and learned, kneeling on his knees he spake these words, the effect whereof here followeth.

O Lord Jesu! which art the only health of all men living, and the everlasting life of them which die in thee, I, wretched sinner, do submit myself wholly unto thy most blessed will; and being sure that the thing cannot perish which is committed unto thy mercy, willingly now I leave this frail and wicked flesh, in sure hope that thou wilt, in better wise, restore it to me again at the last day, in the resurrection of the just. I beseech thee, most merciful Lord Jesu Christ! that thou wilt, by thy grace, make strong my soul against all temptations, and defend me with the buckler of thy mercy against all the assaults of the devil. I see and acknowledge that there is in myself no hope of salvation, but all my confidence, hope, and trust, is in, thy most merciful goodness. I have no merits nor good works which I may allege before thee. Of sins and evil works, alas! I see a great heap; but yet, through thy mercy, I trust to be in the number of them to whom thou wilt not impute their sins; but wilt take and accept me for righteous and just, and to be the inheritor of everlasting life. Thou, merciful Lord! wast born for my sake; thou didst suffer both hunger and thirst for my sake; thou didst teach, pray, and fast for my sake; all thy holy actions and works thou wroughtest for my sake; thou sufferedst most grievous pains and torments for my sake: finally, thou gavest thy most precious body and thy blood to be shed on the cross for my sake. Now, most merciful Saviour! let all these things profit me, that thou freely hast done for me, which hast given thyself also for me. Let thy blood cleanse and wash away the spots and foulness of my sins. Let thy righteousness hide and cover my unrighteousness. Let the merits of thy passion and blood-shedding be satisfaction for my sins. Give me, Lord! thy grace, that the faith of my salvation in thy blood waver not in me, but may ever be firm and constant: that the hope of thy mercy and life everlasting never decay in me: that love wax not cold in me; and finally, that the weakness of my flesh be not overcome with the fear of death. Grant me, merciful Saviour! that when death bath shut up the eyes of my body, yet the eyes of my soul may still behold and look upon thee; and when death bath taken away the use of my tongue, yet my heart may cry and say unto thee, Lord! into thy hands I commend my soul; Lord Jesu I receive my spirit. Amen.

And thus his prayer made, after he had godly and lovingly exhorted them that were about him on the scaffold, he quietly committed his soul into the hands of God; and so patiently suffered the stroke of the axe, by a ragged and butcherly miser, which very ungoodly performed the office.

This valiant soldier and captain of Christ, the aforesaid Lord

Cromwell, as he was most studious of himself in a flagrant zeal to set forward the truth of the gospel, seeking all means and ways to beat down false religion and to advance the true, so he always retained unto him and had about him such as could be found helpers and furtherers of the same; in the number of whom were sundry and divers fresh and quick wits, pertaining to his family; by whose industry and ingenious labours, divers and excellent ballads and books were contrived and set abroad, concerning the suppression of the pope and all popish idolatry.

HOLINSHED'S CHRONICLE (1577)

Raphael Holinshed (c.1525–1580?) was an English chronicler, whose *The Chronicles of England, Scotlande, and Irelande*, usually known as *Holinshed's Chronicles*, was a pioneering attempt to tell the complete history of the country. His work was extensively drawn upon by Shakespeare and other writers. Different editions were published in 1577 and 1587. This passage from the 1577 edition tells of Cromwell's execution, before looking back at his life. As the writer acknowledges, he uses Hall (see Chapter 15) and Foxe (see Chapter 20) as sources.

The ninetenth of July, Tho. L. Cromwell, The Lorde Cromwell late made Earle of Essex, as in the last yeare yee may reade, beeing nowe in the counsel chamber, was suddainely apprehended, & committed to ye Tower of London, which his misfortune many lamented, but mo rejoiced thereat, specially suche as either had bin religious men... The nineteenth of July, he was by Parliamente atteinted, & never came to his aunswere, both of heresie & high treason, as in ye record it appeareth.

The 28 day of Iuly, he was brought to the scaffold on the Tower hill, where he spake these words following.

'I am come hither to die, and not to purge my selfe as may

happen, some think yt I will, for if I shoulde so doe, I were a verye wretch and miser. I am by the law condemned to die, and thanke my L. God, that hath appointed me this death for mine offence, for sithens the time yt I came to yeares of discretion, I haue lyued a sinner, and offended my L. God, for ye whiche I aske him hartily forgiuenes. And it is not unknowen to manye of you, that I haue bene a great traveyler in the worlde, and being but of a base degree, was called to high estate, and sithens the time I came thereunto, I haue offended my prince, for the which I aske him hartily forgivenesse, and besech you al to pray to God with me, that he wil forgive me, O father forgive me, O sonne forgive me, O holy Ghost forgive me, O three persons in one God forgive me, and nowe I pray you that be here, to beare me recorde, I die in the Catholike faith, not doubting in anye article of my faith, no nor doubting in any sacrament of the church. Many have standred me, and reported that I haue bin a bearer of such as have mainteined evil opinions, which is untrue, but I confesse, ye like as God by his holy spirite doth instruct us in the truth, so the devil is ready to seduce us, and I haue bin seduced: but beare me witnesse, that I die in the Catholike faith of the holy Churche, and I hartily desire you to pray for the kings grace, that he may long live with you in health and prosperitie, and after him that his sonne prince Edward, that goodly impe may long raigne over you. And once againe, I desire you to pray for me, that so long as life remaineth in this fleshe. I waver nothing in my faith.'

And then made he his prayer, which was long, but not so long as godly and learned, and after committed his soule to the hands of God & so patiently suffered the stroke of the axe, by a ragged and butcherly miser, which evil favouredly performed the office.

This man beeyng borne in Putney, a village in surrey by the Thaimes side, four miles distant from London, was sonne to a smith, after whose deceasse, hys mother was maried to a shereman: but notwithstanding, the basenesse of his birth and lacke of maintenance was at the beginning (as it happeneth to many other) a great let and hinderance for vertue to shew hir selfe, yet through a singular excel-lencie of wit joined with an industrious diligence of mind, and bely of knowledge, gathered by painefull travaile, and marking the courses of states and gouernements as wel of his native country at home, as in foraine parties abroade, he grewe to suche a sufficient ripenesse of understanding & skill, in ordering of weightie affaires, that he was thought apt and fitte to anye roomth or office whereunto he should be admitted, which being apperteined of the Cardinall of Yorke Wolsey, he tooke him to his service, and making him his solicitor, imployd him aboute busines oftentimes of most importance, wherein he acquit himselfe with suche dexteritie, as aunswered always the credite committed to hym. After the Cardinals fall, he was advanced to ye Kings service, behaving himselfe so advisedly in matters whiche he tooke in hande, that within a small time he rose to high authoritie, and was admitted to be of the privie Counsell, bearyng most rule of all other under the king, as partely ye have hearde, so that by him it well appeared, that the excellencie of beroy call vertues, whyche advance menne to fame and honour, resteth not only in birth and bloud, as a privilege appropriate, and all onely annexed to noble houses, but remaineth at the disposition of the Almightye God, the giver and disposer of all giftes, who reyseth the poore many times from the basest degre, and setteth him up with Printes.

Neverthelesse, concerning the Lorde Cromwell Earle of Essex, if we shal consider his comming up to such high degree of honor as he atteined unto, wee maye doubte whether there be cause more to marvell at his good fortune, or at his worthy and industrious demeanor. But sith in the Booke of actes and monuments yee maye find a sufficient discourse hereof, we neede not to spende more time aboute it, save only as maister Foxe hathe truely noted, such was his actiuitie & forward ripenesse of nature, so ready and pregnant of wit, so discrete and wel advised in judgement... so faithfull and diligent in service, of suche an incomparable memorie, so bold of stomacke and hardie, and coulde doe so wel with his penne, that being conversant in the sight of men, he could not long continue unespyed, nor yet unprovided of favour & help of friends, to set him forward in place and office. Thankeful he was and liberall, not forgetting benefites received, as by his great courtesie shewed to Friscobald the Italian, it well appeared: a favourer of the poore in their sutes, and readye to relieve them that were in daunger to be oppressed by their mightie adversaries: a favourer to ye Gospel, and an enimie to ye pride of Prelates, very shout, and not able well to put up injuries, which wan him shrewde enimies, that ceassed not (as was thoughte) to seeke his overthrowe, till at length they had broght it to passe as they wished. Carefull he was for his servants, and ready to doe them good, so that fearing the thing whiche came to passe, he provided wel for the more part of them, notwithstanding his fall. And thus much for the Lord Cromwell...

The xxviii of Julye as you haue heard before, the Lorde Cromwell was beheaded, and likewise with him the Lorde Hungerford of Heytesburye, who at the houre of his deathe seemed unquiet as many judged hym rather in a frenzie than otherwise: he suffered for buggerie. The thirtieth of July were drawen on hurdles from the Towre to smithfield, Robert Barnes doctor of Divinitie, Thomas Garard, & William Jerome bachelers in divinitie. Jerome was vicar of stepney, and Garard was person of Honylane, also Powell Fetherston, and Abell priests. The firste three were drawne to a stake, there before set up, and were burnt. The other iii were drawne to the galowes, and hanged beheaded and quartred. The three first as is founde in their atteynder, were executed for divers heresies, but none alledged, whereat (sayeth Hall) I have muche mervayled, that their heresies were so manie, and not one alledged as a speciall cause of their death: and verily at their deathes they asked the sheriffes what was their offence for whiche they wer condemned? who answered, they could not tell: but most men sayd it was for preaching against the doctrine of stephen Gardiner bishop of Winchester, who chiefly (as the same Hall sayth) procured their deaths. The last iii to wit, Powel, Fetherston and Abell suffred for treason, as in their atteinder was special mention made, to wit, for denying the kings supremacie, and affirming his marriage with the Lady Catherine Dowager to be good.

STOW'S SURVEY OF LONDON (1603)

John Stow (1524/25–1605) was an English historian and antiquarian, best known for his *A Survey of London*, published in 1598 and then revised in 1603. He also compiled numerous chronicles of English history. Here he tells some brief anecdotes of Cromwell, whose property plans affected Stow's father, including a reference to the Great Muster (see Chapters 6 and 15).

On the south side and at the West end of [Austin Friars' Church], many fayre houses are builded, namely in Throgmorton streete, one very large and spacious, builded in the place of olde and small Tenementes by Thomas Cromwell, Maister of the kinges Jewell house, after that Maister of the Rols, then Lord Cromwell knight Lord privie seale, Vicker Generall, Earle of Essex, high Chamberlaine of England, &c. This house being finished, and having some reasonable plot of ground left for a Garden, hee caused the pales of the Gardens adjoyning to the north parte thereof on a sodaine to bee taken downe, 22. foot to bee measured forth right into the north of every mans ground, a line there to bee drawne, a trench to be cast, a foundation laid, and a high bricke Wall to bee builded. My Father had a Garden there, and an house standing close to his south pale, this house they lowsed from the ground, & bare upon Rowlers into my Fathers Garden 22. foot, ere my Father heard thereof, no warning was given him, nor other answere, when he spake to the surveyers of that worke, but that their Mayster sir Thomas commaunded them so to doe, no man durst go to argue the matter, but each man lost his land, and my Father payde his whole rent, which was vi.s. viii.d. the yeare, for that halfe which was left. Thus much of mine owne knowledge have I thought good to note, that the suddaine rising of some men, causeth them to forget themselves.

These as all other of their times gave great relief to the poore: I my selfe, in that declining time of charity, have oft seene at the Lord Cromwels gate in London, more then two hundered persons served twise every day with bread, meate and drinke sufficient, for hee observed that auncient and charitable custome as all prelates, noble men, or men of honour and worship his predecessors had done before him...

To ende of Orders and Customes in this Citie: also of great families kept by honourable persons thither repayring. And of charitable almes of olde time given, I say for conclusion, that all noble persons, and other of honour and worship, in former times lodging in this Citie, or liberties thereof, did without grudging beare their parts in charges with the Citizens, according to their estimated estates, as I have before said, and could prove by examples, but let men call to minde sir Thomas Cromwel then Lord privie Seale, and Vicker generall, lying in the Citie of London, hee bare his charges to the great muster there, in Anno 1539. he sent his men in great number to the Miles ende, and after them their armour in Carres, with their coates of white cloth, the armes of this Citie. to wit, a red crosse, and a sword on the breast, and backe, which armour and coates they ware amongst the Citizens, without any difference, and marched through the Citie to Westminster.

APPENDIX A: CAVENDISH'S METRICAL VISIONS (1550S)

George Cavendish (see Chapter 18) wrote a series of 'Metrical Visions', moralising poems about historical figures. These were first published in 1825 alongside his *Life of Wolsey*, and presumably also date from the late 1550s.

> *Another there was, of whome I neds must tell:*
> *Cromwell ; all men hyme knewe as well as I :*
> *Which in my mynd all others dyd excell*
> *In extort power and insacyat tyrannye.*
> *First advanced to be the kyng's secretarye,*
> *And next set uppe on the toppe of the whele,*
> *Made Erle of Essex and Lord privye seale.*

CROMWELL, ERLE OF ESSEX

Than began he to speke: Such was myn adventure
To be placed, quod he, in hyghe dignytie,
Wenyng [supposing] my authoritie ever to endure,
And never to be trobled with non adversitie;
But, I perceyve, with royal egles a kight may not flie;

Allthoughe a jay may chatter in a golden cage,
Yet will the eagles disdayne hys parentage.

I rayned and ruled in hyghe estimacion,
From office to office assendyng the degrees;
First in the privye councell was my foundacion,
And cheife secretary with all vantages and fees:
Than folowed me sewters like a swarme of bees.
Thus began fortune on me for to smyle;
I trusted hir so myche that she dyd me begyle.

The title of vice-gerent I had in my style,
Governor of the prelacye and of the lawes devyne;
Also master of the rolls I was, in short while;
Thus began my glory to florish and to shyne,
As thoughe fortune wold hir whele to me resigne :
Unto the state of baron she did me than advaunce,
And next to an erle: thus was fortune's chaunce.

In this hyghe estate I myght not long endure,
Fortune did so chaynge hir favorable chere;
She slipte away all sodenly as it hathe byn her ure,
Hir covert countenance dyd than to me appere;
I trusted hir to myche, I bought hir trust to dere;
She promysed me so fayer, that I could not beware
Of hir disceytfull bayte, till I was in hir snare.

To Aman the Agagite I may be compared,
That invented lawes God's people to confound;
And for Mardocheus a galhowsse he prepared,
To hang him theron, if he myght be found,
Which he erected fyvetye [50] cubytts from the ground,
Wheron Mardocheus to hang was all his trust,
Yet was hymself hanged on theme first.

So wrought I, alas! with the lawes of this realme,
Devised a law ayenst the accused,
Condempnyng without answere, or he could understand
The ground of his offence, it myght not be refused;
Thus straytly the lawes my subtill wytt abused:
Therfor, oon of the first, I ame tastyng on the payn;
Such measure I measured is measured me again.

I may therfore conclude, experience hath me taught
All is but vayn that man doth here invent;
Ther worldly wytt God bryngyth oft to naught,
And with ther workes he is not well content.
Behold my deads, than may you se it evydent,
That for my presumption, wanting Goddis grace,
My lyfe consumed is within a short space.

This is thend of my complaynt, I must therfor depart;
Farewell, my frends ! farewell, my foos [foes] all ;
Take of me ensample and plant it in your hart,
That suche lyke fortune may geve you a lyke fall;
Consider well, therfor, that here ye be mortall:
All thyng hath an end, whye do ye honors crave?
Whan ye shall, as I ame, be covered with your grave.

Thys late Lord Cromwell may warne you all
That foremost ride aloft in the chayer,
Not to trust to fortune, that tomblethe as a ball,
For chaunces uncerteyn, that often fall onware...

APPENDIX B: THE LIFE AND DEATH OF THOMAS LORD CROMWELL(1602)

Thomas Lord Cromwell is a history play first published in 1602, although some scholars have suggested it was written as early as 1582–3. It was attributed to 'W.S.', leading many to believe it is an apocryphal work by Shakespeare, but numerous other authors have been suggested, and it is not officially regarded as part of the Shakespearean canon. The play begins with the young Cromwell complaining that the noise of his father's smithies is disturbing his studies. Below are a few extracts showing how Cromwell's personality is presented; the full text can be found online (see Bibliography).

Act 1 Scene 2

> Why should my birth keep down my mounting spirit?
> Are not all creatures subject unto time?
> To time, who doth abuse the world,
> And fills it full of hodge-podge bastardy;
> There's legions now of beggars on the earth,
> That their original did spring from Kings,
> And many Monarchs now, whose Fathers were

The riffe-raffe of their age; for time and fortune
Weares out a noble train to beggery;
And from the Dunghill minions doe advance
To state: and mark, in this admiring world
This is but course, which in the name of Fate
Is seen as often as it whirles about:
The River *Thames* that by our door doth passe,
His first beginning is but small and shallow,
Yet keeping on his course growes to a Sea.
And likewise *Wolsey*, the wonder of our age,
His birth as mean as mine, a Butchers Son;
Now who within this Land a greater man?
Then, *Cromwell*, cheer thee up, and tell thy soul,
That thou may'st live to flourish and controule.

Act 2 Scene 1

(*Cromwell is working as a merchant's clerk in Antwerp; the play also refers to his travels in France, Spain, Germany and Italy.*)

Thus far my reckoning doth go straight & even.
But, *Cromwell*, this same plodding sits not thee;
Thy mind is altogether set on travel,
And not to live thus cloystered, like a Nun;
It is not this same trash, that I regard,
Experience is the jewel of my heart.

Act 4 Scene 0

(*The chorus speaks.*)

Now *Cromwells* highest fortunes doth begin.
Wolsey that lov'd him, as he did his life:

Committed all his treasure to his hands,
Wolsey is dead, and *Gardiner* his man
Is now created Bishop of *Winchester*:
Pardon if we omit all *Wolsey's* life,
Because our play depends on *Cromwells* death,
Now sit and see his highest state of all;
His height of rising: and his sodain fall,
Pardon the errors is already past,
And live in hope the best doth come at last:
My hope upon your favour doth depend,
And look to have your liking ere the end.

Act 4 Scene 1

(In this scene Cromwell has multiple honours bestowed upon him. Stephen Gardiner (1483–1555), the Bishop of Winchester and no fan of Cromwell in real life, emerges as his arch-enemy here.)

But *Gardiner* means his glory shall be dim'd:
Shall *Cromwell* live a greater man then I?
My envy with his honour now is bred,
I hope to shorten *Cromwell* by the head.

Act 4 Scene 2

(The argument between Gardiner and Cromwell which leads the former to scheme for the latter's execution; there is no mention of Henry's disaffection with Anne of Cleves as the cause of Cromwell's downfall.)

Crom. Good morrow to my Lord of *Winchester*:
I know you bear me hard, about the Abbey lands.
Gard. Have I not reason, when Religion is wronged?
You had no colour for what you have done.

Crom. Yes, the abolishing of Antichrist,
And of his Popish order from our Realm:
I am no enemy to Religion,
But what is done, it is for *England*'s good:
What did they serve for, but to feed a sort
Of lazy Abbots, and of full-fed Fryers?
They neither plow, nor sow, and yet they reap
The fat of all the Land, and suck the poor:
Look what was theirs, is in King *Henrie*'s hands,
His wealth before lay in the Abbey lands.
Gard. Indeed these things you have alledg'd, my Lord,
When, God doth know, the infant yet unborn,
Will curse the time, the Abbies were pul'd down:
I pray now where is Hospitality?
Where now may poor distressed people go,
For to relieve their need, or rest their bones,
When weary travel doth oppress their limmes?
And where religious men should take them in,
Shall now be kept back by a Mastive dog...

APPENDIX C: THE LEGEND OF GREAT CROMWELL (1607)

This poem by Michael Drayton (1563–1631) was first published in 1607. He uses Foxe's account of Cromwell (see Chapter 20) as his main source, and probably the play by 'W.S.' (see Appendix B). The full poem runs to almost 1,000 lines; below are some extracts.

> Awak'd, and trembling betwixt Rage and Dread
> With the lowd slander (by the impious Time)
> That of my Actions everywhere is spred,
> Through which to honour falsly I should clime:
> From the sad dwelling of th'untimely dead,
> To quit Me of that Execrable Crime,
> CROMWELL appeares, his wretched plight to show,
> Much that can tell, as one that much did know.

> Roughly not made up in the common mould,
> That with the vulgar vilely I should die,
> What thing so strange of CROMWELL is not told?
> What man more prays'd? Who more condemn'd than I?
> That with the World when I am waxed old,
> Most't were unfit that Fame of Me should lie,

With Fables vaine my Historie to fill,
Forcing my good, excusing of my Ill.

...

Putney the Place made blessed by my Birth,
Whose meanest Cottage simply Me did shrowd,
To Me as dearest of the English Earth;
So of my bringing that poore Village proud,
Though in a time when never lesse the Dearth
Of happie Wits, yet Mine so well allow'd,
That with the best She boldly durst prefer
Me, that my breath acknowledged from Her.

Twice flow'd proud Thames as at my comming wood,
Striking the wondring Bord'rers with Feare,
And the pale Genius of that aged floud,
To my sicke Mother labouring did appeare,
And with a Countenance much distracted stood,
Threatning the Fruit Her pained Wombe should beare:
My speedy Birth being added thereunto,
Seem'd to fore-tell, that much I came to doe.

...

Whilst yet my Father by His painfull Trade,
Whose labour'd Anvile only was His Fee,
Whom my great tow'rdnesse strongly did perswade,
In Knowledge to have educated Mee:
But Death did Him unluckily invade,
Ere He the fruits of His Desire could see,
Leaving Me young, then little that did know,
How Me the Heavens had purpos'd to bestow.

Hopelesse as helplesse most might Me suppose,
Whose meannesse seem'd their abject breath to draw:
Yet did my Brest that glorious fire inclose,
Which their dull purblind Ignorance not saw,
Which still is settled upon outward Showes,
The Vulgars judgement ever is so raw,
Which the unworthiest sottishly doe love,
In their owne Region properly that move.

...

But when my meanes to faile me I did find,
My selfe to Travell presently I tooke,
For 'twas distastefull to my Noble mind,
That the vile World into my wants should looke,
Being besides industriously inclinde,
To measure others Actions with my Booke,
My Judgement more to rectifie thereby,
In matters that were difficult and hye.

When, loe, it hapt, that Fortune as my Guide,
Of me did with such providence dispose,
That th' English Merchants then, who did reside
At Antwerpe, me their Secretarie chose,
(As though in me to manifest her pride)
Whence to those Principalities I rose,
To plucke me downe, whence afterward shee fear'd,
Beyond her Power, that almost shee had rear'd.

When first the wealthy Netherlands me trayn'd,
In wise Commerce most proper to that Place,
And from my Countrie carefully me wayn'd,
As with the World it meant to winne me Grace,
Where great experience happily I gayn'd;
Yet here I seem'd but tutor'd for a space,

For high imployment otherwise ordayn'd,
Till which, the Time I idlely entertayn'd.

For Boston businesse hotly then in hand,
The charge thereof on CHAMBERS being layd,
Comming to Flanders, hapt to understand
Of me, whom he requested him to ayd;
Of which, when I the benefit had scand,
Weighing what time at Antwerpe I had stayd,
Soone it me wonne faire Italy to trie,
Under a cheerefull and more luckie skie:

...

And my experience happily me taught
Into the secrets of those Times to see,
From whence to England afterward I brought
Those slights of State deliv'red there to mee,
In t'which there then were very few that sought,
Nor did with th'humour of that age agree,
Which after did most fearefull things effect,
Whose secret working few did then suspect.

...

Making my selfe to mightie Woolsey knowne,
That ATLAS , which the governement upstay'd,
Who from meane place in little time was growne
Up to him, which that weight upon him lay'd,
And being got the neerest to his Throne,
He the more easly this great Kingdome sway'd,
Leaning thereon his wearied selfe to breathe,
Whil'st even the Greatest sat him farre beneath.

Where learned MORE and GARDINER I met,
Men, in those Times, immatchable for wit,
Able that were the dullest Spirit to whet,
And did my humour excellently fit,
Into their Ranke and worthily did get
There as their proud Competitor to sit.
One Excellence to many is the Mother,
Wits doe, as Creatures, one beget another.

This Founder of the Palaces of Kings,
Whose Veines with more then usuall Spirit were fild,
A Man ordayned to the mighti'st Things,
In Oxford then determining to build
To CHRIST a Colledge, and together brings
All that thereof the great Foundation wills,
There me imployes, whose industrie he found
Worthy to worke upon the noblest Ground.

Yet in the entrance wisely did he feare
Coyne might fall short, yet with this worke on fire,
Wherefore such Houses as Religious were,
Whose being no necessitie require,
But that the greater very well might beare,
From Rome the Card'nall cunningly did hire,
Winning withall his Soveraigne to consent,
It colouring with so Holy an intent.

...

Whil'st to the King continually I sue,
And in this businesse faithfully did stirre,
Strongly t'approve my judgement to be true,
'Gainst those who most supposed me to erre,
Nor the least meanes which any way I knew
Might grace me, or my purposes preferre

Did I omit, till I had wonne his Eare,
Most that me mark'd, when least he seem'd to heare.

...

For first from Knighthood rising in degree,
The Office of the Jewell-house my lot,
After, the Rolles he frankly gave to Me,
From whence a Privie Counseller I got,
Then of the Garter: and then Earle to be
Of Essex: yet sufficient these were not,
But to the great Vicegerencie I grew,
Being a Title as Supreme as new.

So well did Me these Dignities befit,
And Honour so Me every way became,
As more then Man, I had beene made for it,
Or as from Me it had deriv'd the Name:
Where was he found? whose love I not requit,
Beyond His owne imaginarie aime,
Which had Me succor'd neerely being driven,
As things to Me that idly were not given?

What Tongue so slow, the Tale shall not report
Of Hospitable FRISCOBALD and Mee,
And shew in how reciprocall a sort
My thankes did with his Courtesie agree,
When as my Meanes in Italy were short,
That Me reliev'd, I lesse that would not bee,
When I of England , was Vicegerent made,
His former Bounties lib'rally repaid?

...

Those secret Foes yet subt'ly to deceive,
That me maligning, lifted at my State,
The King to marry forward still I heave,
(His former Wife being repudiate)
With ANNE, the Sister of the Duke of Cleave ,
The German Princes to confederate,
To backe me still 'gainst those against me lay,
Which as their owne retayn'd me here in pay.

Which my destruction principally wrought,
When afterward abandoning her bed,
Which to his will to passe could not be brought,
So long as yet I bare about my head,
The only Man her safetie that had sought,
Of her againe and only favoured,
Which was the cause he hasted to my end,
Upon whose fall Hers likewise did depend.

For in his high distemp'rature of blood,
Who was so Great, whose Life he did regard?
Or what was it that his desires withstood,
He not invested, were it ne'r so hard?
Nor held he me so absolutely good,
That though I crost him, I could not be spar'd,
But with those things I lastly was to goe,
Which he to ground did violently throw.

When WINCHESTER , with all those Enemies,
Whom my much power from Audience had debarr'd,
The longer time their mischiefes to devise,
Feeling with me how lastly now it far'd,
When I had done the King what did suffice,
Lastly thrust in against me to be heard,
When what was ill, contrarily turn'd good,
Making amayne to th'sheading of my blood.

And that the King his action doth deny,
And on my guilt doth altogether lay,
Having his Ryot satisfied thereby,
Seemes not to know how I therein did sway,
What late was Truth, now turn'd to Heresie:
When he by me had purchased his prey,
Himselfe to cleere, and satisfie the sin,
Leaves me but late his instrument therein.

Those Lawes I made my selfe alone to please,
To give me power more freely to my Will,
Even to my Equals hurtfull sundrie wayes,
(Forced to things that most doe say were ill)
Upon me now as violently seyze,
By which I lastly perisht by my Skill,
On mine owne Necke returning (as my due)
That heavie Yoke wherein by me they drew.

My Greatnesse threatned by ill-boding eyes,
My actions strangely censured of all,
Yet in my way, my giddinesse not sees
The Pit wherein I likely was to fall:
O were the sweets of mans felicities
Often amongst not temp'red with some Gall!
He would forget by his o'rweening skill,
Just Heaven above doth censure good and ill.

Things over ranke, doe never kindly beare,
As in the Corne, the Fluxure when we see
Fills but the Straw, when it should feede the Eare,
Rotting that time, in ripening it should bee,
And being once downe, it selfe can never reare:
With us well doth this Simile agree,
(By the Wise man) due to the Great in all,
By their owne weight being broken in their fall.

Selfe-loving Man what sooner doth abuse,
And more then his prosperitie doth wound?
Into the deepe but fall, how can he chuse
That over-strides whereon his foote to ground?
Who sparingly prosperitie doth use,
And to himselfe doth after-ill propound,
Unto his height who happily doth clime,
Sits above Fortune, and controlleth Time.

Not choosing what us most delight doth bring,
And most that by the generall breath is freed,
Wooing that Suffrage, but the vertuous Thing,
Which in it selfe is excellent indeed,
Of which the depth and perfect managing
Amongst the most, but few there be that heed,
Affecting that agreeing with their blood,
Seldome enduring, and as seldome good.

But whil'st we strive too suddenly to rise
By flatt'ring Princes with a servill tong,
And being Soothers to their tyrannies,
Worke our much woes by what doth many wrong,
And unto others tending injuries,
Unto our selves it hapning oft among.
In our owne Snares unluckily are caught,
Whil'st our attempts fall instantly to naught.

The Councell Chamber place of my Arrest,
Where chiefe I was, when greatest was the store,
And had my speeches noted of the best,
That did them as high Oracles adore:
A Parliament was lastly my Enquest,
That was my selfe a Parliament before,
The Towre-Hill Scaffold last I did ascend:
Thus the great'st Man of England made his end.

BIBLIOGRAPHY

- Bandello, M., *The novels of Matteo Bandello, bishop of Agen* (ed. J. Payne), Villon Society, 1890.
- Borman, T., *Thomas Cromwell: The untold story of Henry VIII's most faithful servant*, Hodder & Stoughton, 2015
- Cavendish, G., *The Life of Cardinal Wolsey and Metrical Visions* (2 vols), ed. S.W.Singer, Harding, Triphook and Lepard, 1825
- Foxe, J., *Actes and Monuments of the Church*, John Day, 1563
- Froude, J.A., *History of England* (Vol. 3), Longmans, Green & Co., 1893.
- Gee, H. & Hardy, J.W., *Documents Illustrative of English Church History*, Macmillan, 1914.
- Hall, E., *Henry VIII* (from *Hall's Chronicle*), T.C. & E.C. Jack, 1904.
- Harpsfield, N. & Roper, W., *Lives of Saint Thomas More* (ed. E.E. Reynolds), Everyman's Library (Dent), 1963
- Holinshed, R., *Holinshed's Chronicles of England, Scotland, and Ireland, 1577*, available at http://www.cems.ox.ac.uk/holinshed/
- Hume, M.A.S. (ed.), *Chronicle of King Henry VIII. of England:*

Being a Contemporary Record of Some of the Principal Events of the Reigns of Henry VIII and Edward VI (The Spanish Chronicle), G. Bell and sons, 1889.

- Hutchinson, R., *Thomas Cromwell: The Rise and Fall of Henry VIII's Most Notorious Minister*, Weidenfeld & Nicholson, 2009.
- *Letters and Papers, Foreign and Domestic, Henry VIII*, various volumes (ed. J.S. Brewer, J. Gairdner et al.), 1875; online at https://www.british-history.ac.uk/search/series/letters-papers-hen8
- Loades, D., *Thomas Cromwell: Servant to Henry VIII*, Amberley Publishing, 2014.
- MacCulloch, D., *Thomas Cromwell: A Life*, Allen Lane, 2018.
- Merriman, R.B., *Life and Letters of Thomas Cromwell* (2 vols), Clarendon Press, 1902.
- Moorhouse, G., *The Pilgrimage of Grace: The Rebellion that Shook King Henry VIII's Throne*, Phoenix, 2003.
- Phillips, T., *The History of the Life of Reginald Pole*, William Jackson, 1765.
- Schofield, J., *The Rise & Fall of Thomas Cromwell: Henry VIII's Most Faithful Servant*, The History Press, 2011.
- Stow, J., *A Survey of London. Reprinted From the Text of 1603* (ed. C.L. Kingsford), Oxford, 1908; available at http://www.british-history.ac.uk/no-series/survey-of-london-stow/1603
- Tillotson, K., 'Michael Drayton as a "Historian" in the "Legend of Cromwell"', *The Modern Language Review*, Vol. 34, No. 2 (April 1939).
- Wriothesley, C., *A chronicle of England during the reigns of the Tudors, from A.D. 1485 to 1559* (Vol. 1, ed. W.D. Hamilton), Camden Society, 1875–77.
- W.S., *The History of the Life and Death of Thomas Lord Cromwell*, 1603; 1664 folio available at https://internetshakespeare.uvic.ca/doc/Cro_F3/index.html

Printed in Great Britain
by Amazon